COMPETENCY ASSESSMENT FIELD GUIDE

A Real World Guide for Implementation and Application

DONNA WRIGHT

CREATIVE HEALTH CARE MANAGEMENT

COMPETENCY ASSESSMENT FIELD GUIDE

Copyright © 2015 by Donna Wright

All rights reserved. No part of this book may be reproduced in any form or by any electronic or mechanical means, including information storage and retrieval systems, without permission in writing from the publisher, except by a reviewer who may quote brief passages in a review.

Library of Congress Cataloging-in-Publication Data

Wright, Donna, author. Competency assessment field guide : a real world guide for implementation and application / Donna Wright.
     p. ; cm.
 Includes bibliographical references and index.
 ISBN 978-1-886624-90-0 (softcover : alk. paper) — ISBN 978-1-886624-91-7 (ebook)
 I. Title.
 [DNLM: 1. Professional Competence--standards--Case Reports. 2. Employee Performance Appraisal--methods--Case Reports. 3. Health Facility Administration--methods--Case Reports. 4. Personnel Management--methods--Case Reports. 5. Quality Assurance, Health Care--Case Reports. W 21]
 R729.5.H4
 362.1068--dc23
                           2015011819

Softcover ISBN 13: 978-1-886624-90-0
ebook ISBN 13: 978-1-886624-91-7

Printed and bound in the United States of America

21 20 19 18 17   9 8 7 6 5

Fifth Printing: October 2017

Cover and interior design by James Monroe Design, LLC.

Cover artwork by Donna Wright

For permission and ordering information, write to:
6200 Baker Road, Suite 200
Minneapolis, MN 55346

chcm@chcm.com
800.728.7766 / 952.854.9015

Dedication

This book is dedicated to all of the health care professionals who are courageous enough to not just go along with comments like, "We've always done it this way," or "They told us we needed to do it like this." Instead, these brave professionals reached out to seek strategies that create truly healthy systems that will have a positive impact on patients, employees, and organizations, while consistently achieving excellence in a highly regulated world. I thank them for their innovation and tenacity in finding better ways. I thank them for their courage to "boldly go where no one has gone before!"

Table of Contents

About the Author ix
Acknowledgements xi
Introduction 1
Overview of the Wright Competency Assessment Model 5

SECTION A
Answers to the Most Frequently Asked Questions about Competency Assessment

    Regulations and Standards 13

    Float Pool Competencies 17

    Checklists vs. "Checklists" 23

    Competent Person vs. Competent Action 25

    Avoiding "Spray and Pray": Education is Not Always the Answer 29

    What Every Educator and Professional Development Specialist
    Needs to Know 33

    Validators 35

    Competencies Can be Used as the Second Half of the Job Description 39

    Performance Review and Competency Assessment:
    How Do they Fit Together? 41

    Standardization vs. Sameness 43

    Automating Our Competency Process: Tracking, Documentation,
    and Communication 45

    Competency and Engagement 49

SECTION B
Reflections from Organizations that have Used the Wright Competency Model

    Introduction 57

Stories from the Field

    A Journey to Competency Brings a Culture Change
    Waterbury Hospital
    Waterbury, Connecticut 61

    Competency as the Key to a Nursing Practice Model
    Lawrence Memorial Hospital
    Lawrence, Kansas 65

    From Fragmentation to Consistency and Alignment
    Buena Vista Regional Medical Center
    Storm Lake, Iowa 69

    Maximum Staff Involvement Creates its Own Momentum
    Kettering Behavioral Medical Center
    Kettering, Ohio 73

    The Goal Was Saving Resources; the Outcome Was a Valuable Competency
    Process
    UnityPoint Health Des Moines
    Des Moines, Iowa 77

    A Very Diverse System Plus Regulatory Requirements for
    Education Required a Streamlined System
    Norton Healthcare
    Louisville, Kentucky 81

    From Education as the Solution to Every Performance Problem,
    to Demonstrating the Skills Needed to Do the Job
    North Kansas City Hospital
    North Kansas City, Missouri 85

    Discovering the True Meaning of Competency Makes for Authentic,
    Rewarding Assessment
    St. Luke's Health System
    Boise, Idaho 89

    A Story of Cost Savings ... and Tenacity!
    St. Luke's Children's Hospital
    Boise, Idaho 93

TABLE OF CONTENTS

A Paradigm Shift (and a Creative Automotive Theme) Brought Accountability and Engagement
Children's Mercy Hospital
Kansas City, Missouri 95

"We Now Talk in Competency Language"
Virginia Commonwealth University Health System
Richmond, Virginia 101

A Program that Truly Validates Competency also Enhances the Patient Experience, Patient Safety, and Nurse Satisfaction
Morton Plant Mease Health Care (part of BayCare Health System)
Clearwater, Florida 105

Designing a Skills Fair that Actually Assesses Skills
Morton Plant Hospital
Clearwater, Florida 115

Decentralized, Time-Sensitive Competency Education
Robert Wood Johnson University Hospital at Somerset
Somerville, New Jersey 117

Placing Accountability for Competency Verification with the Professional Nurse Elevates Practice throughout the Organization
Avera McKennan Hospital & University Health Center
Sioux Falls, South Dakota 121

A Change in Competency Assessment Improves Staff Unity
University of Pennsylvania Health System
Philadelphia, Pennsylvania 125

Results and Outcomes

Billings Clinic
Billings, Montana 131

Fairfield Medical Center
Lancaster, Ohio 137

Arkansas Children's Hospital
Little Rock, Arkansas 145

Charles George Veterans Affairs Medical Center
Asheville, North Carolina 153

Baptist Health South Florida
Miami, Florida 161

Sharp Memorial Hospital
San Diego, California 167

SECTION C
Tips for Implementing the Wright Competency Assessment Model

    Where to Start.. 173

    Ongoing Competency Assessment: Planning the Competency Cycle...... 177

    Transition Planning: Implementing a Smooth Transition to
    Get Everyone on Board with the New Competency Model 179

    Leadership Buy-in 183

    The Wright Competency Model: What it Takes to Bring it to Life......... 185

    Competently Go 187

Special Thanks 189

References 193

Index..195

About the Author

Donna Wright is a nurse and professional development specialist. She has a Master's Degree in Nursing Education and is the author of *The Ultimate Guide to Competency Assessment in Health Care* (2005), which has become a world-wide standard in health care competency assessment. *The Ultimate Guide to Competency Assessment in Health Care* has been translated into Japanese and is being used throughout Japan.

Donna is a consultant with Creative Health Care Management in Minneapolis, Minnesota. She has worked on six continents, consulting and speaking on competency assessment and professional development. (The only continent she has not worked on yet is Antarctica . . . the keyword here is "yet.")

Donna is a past president of the Association of Nursing Professional Development (formerly National Nursing Staff Development Organization), and received that organization's Excellence in Consultation award in 1995. She works as a speaker and consultant to help health care organizations create competency programs and systems that go beyond simply meeting regulations to focus on the real reason we do what we do each day—help the patient!

Donna lives in the Black Hills of South Dakota with her husband, Jacques, who also works in health care.

Acknowledgements

This book was inspired by many people in the field of health care education, professional development, talent management, and human resources. Thank you for keeping health care on the cutting edge of excellence every day. Your commitment to our work and to those who deliver it is amazing and often unseen.

Special thanks to the unsung heroes behind this publication:

> Rebecca Smith, developmental lead editor
>
> Marty Lewis-Hunstiger, developmental editor and esteemed nursing colleague
>
> Chris Bjork, publication specialist and resources director
>
> Jay Monroe, graphic specialist, production layout, and cover design
>
> Catherine Perrizo, MBA, editing and data analysis
>
> Melisa Klinkhammer, permissions and proofreading
>
> Kary Gillenwaters, proofreading

Your commitment to the quality of the finished product keeps me focused and honest, and your dedication to helping health care professionals get the information they need inspires me on a daily basis. These projects always require a team. I am glad you are my teammates!

Finally, I'd like to thank the authors from the field, without whom this book would not be a true field guide: Julie Bane, Carla Borchardt, Deborah A. Combs, Sharon Conway, Annette Dailey, Ellen Derry, Carol Dimura, Janet Donnelly, Laurie Ecoff, Solimar Figueroa, Michele Fix, Kitty Hancock, Barbara Johns, Michele Kelly, Ellen Kisling, Michele Kolp, Michelle Lane, Walter Lewanowicz, Paula Lewis, Lynn Marder, Felisha Mason, Sandy Nasshan, Susan Regan O'Brien, Mary Rogers, Rose Schaffer, Michele Schwister, Cherry R. Shogren, Christine Sites, Laurie Smith, Donna Steigleder, Jennifer Tafelmeyer, Belinda Toole, Doris Van Dyke, Lametria Wafford, Tammy Webb, and Robin Wicks.

Introduction

The competency assessment process in any organization tells a great deal about the organization; it is the DNA of who we are as a group. If our competency assessment process is a lot of busy work and the employees find no meaning in it, our organization may have a lack of trust and direction.

We can easily fall into some common competency assessment traps and ruts. Organizations can have some common misconceptions and develop whole systems around ideas and concepts that are weak and even misleading. Some of our current competency assessment processes may be based on some very weak ideas that are not founded on evidence. Frankly, the research in the area of professional development in health care is limited. We in the competency world are just beginning to ground our work in a solid body of research and outcomes. The knowledge is evolving, and it will come.

Misconceptions

Here are a few common misconceptions we often lean on that have little or no proof of making strong competency assessment and in some cases actually have a negative impact on our efforts:

- Competencies need to be reassessed every year (repeating them again and again to make sure people do not lose skill).

- If we check people off (watching them do a task or skill), they are competent to do the procedure.

- Most skills required to do a job in health care are technical in nature (rather than involving critical thinking or interpersonal skills).

- There is a list of mandatory competencies from regulatory bodies that people are required to do every year.

First, I'll offer some basic responses to these common misconceptions. Then, in the rest of this book, I will help you create a healthier approach to competency assessment. I believe that competency assessment can be much more effective when we give ourselves a stable foundation on which to build our efforts. Let's not focus on checking every skill we do every day, but instead work on developing and mastering the skills that need our attention and move us forward to meet the challenges of the future. Our world is changing every day; our competencies need to change to reflect this reality.

> *Our world is changing every day; our competencies need to change to reflect this reality.*

Here are my responses to the common misconceptions that so often provide the foundation for unsatisfying competency assessment efforts:

Misconception One: Competencies need to be reassessed every year (repeating them again and again to make sure people do not lose skill).

Reality Check: There is no research-based evidence showing that people lose skill. Over time, if we do not use a skill, we can get rusty and lack some proficiency, but we do not lose skill. What happens more often is that the environment changes and our skills need to evolve to match the new demands. For example, most people know how to create a document on a computer. I do not wake up one day and say, "Oops, I lost that skill." But someday I may come to work and have trouble using my computer. Is that because I lost skill? No. It is often because someone from the IT department upgraded my computer, and now I have trouble making things work. It's not because I lost skill; it's because the environment changed, and my skills from yesterday no longer match the challenges of today.

Misconception Two: If we check people off (watching them do a task or skill), they are competent to do the procedure.

Reality Check: Competency assessment is often more complex than watching someone demonstrate a task. There is no magic number of demonstrations that makes someone competent (because check marks on checklists do not cause competency). Competency requires knowledge and repetition. Therefore, much of what we will discuss in this book is about outcomes and results. It's about holding the employee accountable, not just for knowing something or for demonstrating it once, but for getting *consistent* results. We are in the early stages of outcome measurements in health care, and we are moving toward the widespread measurement of individual outcomes as well.

Misconception Three: Most skills required to do a job in health care are technical in nature (rather than involving critical thinking or interpersonal skills).

Reality Check: There are three domains of skill—technical, interpersonal, and critical thinking—first identified by Dorothy del Bueno (1980). Most jobs in health care, including everyone from clinical and non-clinical frontline workers to the CEO, require proficiency in all three domains of skill. While the technical aspect of our work is important, we also need to relate to each other (staff, patient, and public); we need to prioritize effectively; we need to document and record; we need to solve problems; etc. All of this takes more than just technical skills. Actually most of our problems come from poor decision making and/or dysfunctional relationships and communication, and competency assessment can and should address those skills as well.

Misconception Four: There is a list of mandatory competencies from regulatory bodies that are required every year.

Reality Check: This is one of the biggest myths out there. Yes, there are many, many regulatory bodies that oversee various aspects of health care. But here is the amazing thing: most regulations point us in a general direction rather than toward specific prescriptive action. These bodies know that "one size does not fit all," so most standards are intent-driven; they ask us to move toward a goal or to pay closer attention to some aspects of our work and outcomes. When I see an organization that has been cited by a regulatory agency for a competency issue, often it is not related to a regulatory standard, but because the organization did not follow its own policies. For example: If a standard asks us to "incorporate restraints into our periodic competency assessment process," that does not necessarily mean we have to do a restraint competency every year. It means we need to pay closer attention to restraints and monitor our outcomes and skills around this area of practice. But, if we write into our internal policy that all employees will do a restraint competency yearly, then they need to do it yearly or we will be cited. We chose to make this *our* policy, and the regulatory body will now hold us accountable to our policy.

> *My advice to everyone is to look over your internal policies, and ask yourselves who wrote them and whether each policy is serving you...or controlling you.*

Besides, if there really were some kind of magic list of mandatory competencies for all health care employees, why it is that when I go to so many hospitals, I see different lists? People within the organization look at the standards, make interpretations and judgment calls, and write policies that are often more stringent than any regulatory standard. My advice to everyone is to look over your internal policies, and ask yourselves who wrote them and whether each policy is serving you . . . or controlling you.

Overview of the Wright Competency Assessment Model

My competency assessment model is based on some basic principles. I believe that competencies should really matter, and that asking people to do a list of competencies as a mandatory ritual without thinking about the relevance and value of each competency is never effective.

Principles that form the foundation of my competency model:

1. Select competencies that matter to both the people involved and to the organization.

    › Competencies should reflect the current realities of practice.

    › Competencies should be connected to quality improvement data.

    › Competencies should be dynamic and collaboratively selected.

    › Competency selection itself involves critical thinking.

2. Select the right verification methods for each competency identified (which may require some outside-the-box thinking).

3. Clarify the roles and accountability of the manager, educator, and employee in the competency process.

4. Employee-centered competency verification creates a culture of engagement and commitment. It is the center of the model. See **Figure I.1** on the following page.

Figure I.1: Wright Competency Model Elements of Success

This competency model is grounded in three principles – ownership, empowerment, and accountability.

Ownership

In order to create and foster a deep sense of ownership of the competency assessment process, competencies should be identified for each cycle in a collaborative way by a group at the unit or department level. Who needs to be at the table to do this? Certainly, the manager and some employees. The manager is ultimately accountable for competency assessment (legally and in order to be in compliance with many regulatory standards), so he or she needs to be at the table for this step. Employees are key players in the determination of competencies and how they will be measured, because the employees know the job better than anybody else. By collaborating broadly to select the competencies for each assessment period, you are creating ownership in the outcomes and practices in a given area.

> *By collaborating broadly to select the competencies for each assessment period, you are creating ownership in the outcomes and practices in a given area.*

Competencies for each cycle should be selected based on the current needs of the organization and of the job. See **Figure I.2** on the following page.

OVERVIEW OF THE WRIGHT COMPETENCY ASSESSMENT MODEL

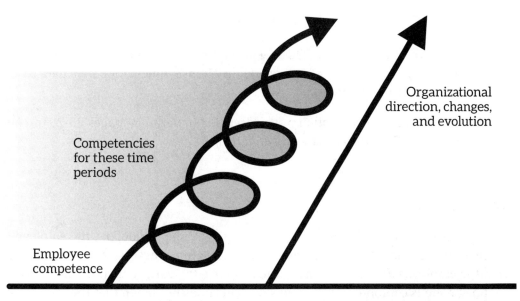

Figure I.2: Competency Evolution and Organizational Evolution

Employees need to come to the organization with the skills needed to start the job or a willingness to gain these skills quickly in orientation. However, because the competencies for each job class will evolve as the organization evolves, competencies need to be periodically assessed. In most organizations, "periodically" has been defined as yearly. Repeating the same list of competencies every year is ineffective for a number of reasons.

1. The world changes, and new skills (in all three domains—technical, interpersonal, and critical thinking) are needed in order for people to maintain proficiency.

2. A repetitive, everything-but-the-kitchen-sink list of competencies can be perceived as a disrespectful waste of time and can damage morale, while a carefully chosen list of highly relevant competencies can improve morale.

3. A carefully chosen list of highly relevant competencies helps people feel capable, engaged, and energized in their work. (Section B of this book will provide ample evidence of this phenomenon!)

Competencies should be identified or selected for each cycle based on four main categories of inquiry:

1. What in the job class is NEW?

2. What in the job class is CHANGING?

3. What are the HIGH RISK aspects of the job?

4. What are the PROBLEMATIC aspects currently seen in the outcomes for the job class? (This step links quality improvement/outcome data to competency assessment.)

These four categories of inquiry are described in detail on pages 23-29 of *The Ultimate Guide to Competency Assessment in Health Care*.

Empowerment

Once the competencies are selected for a given time period, put the employee at the center of the verification process for competency assessment. This means that the employee will need to bring the evidence forward that shows or verifies that he or she is competent in a given skill. This does not mean that the employee can select whatever verification method he or she wants to use. We may ask an employee to show/prove that he or she can use a defibrillator. The employee cannot just choose "self-assessment" to show/prove this skill. Selection of verification methods is an element of competency assessment in which the educator has a key role. Some competencies may have three or four possible verification methods. The key is to give the employee choices for each competency and then ask the employee to bring the evidence forward to the organization. This puts empowerment into the process, as well as providing a measurement of commitment. By not making any effort to bring evidence forward, an employee clearly demonstrates a lack of commitment to the competency process. Follow-up action for this employee issue would be, not further education and training, but action addressing a lack of engagement and commitment.

> *Once the competencies are selected for a given time period, put the employee at the center of the verification process for competency assessment.*

Accountability

In the competency assessment process, the role of leaders (managers, educators, human resources personnel, and others) is not to run around checking off employees or to spoon-feed the process to them. Instead, our role is to set up a process in which the organization's mission (patient care) is the driving force behind our efforts AND the employee is fully supported in getting things done to achieve it. We do this by giving employees clear direction and support. We ask periodically, "How are you doing with your competency verification? If you have any problems let us (your leaders) know." What we do not do is spoon-feed people and treat them like children. Articulate the expectations for the time period, support people in accomplishing the goal, eliminate any barriers they may identify, and then hold them accountable if the goal is not met. This creates a healthy work environment by sending the clear message, "You as an employee will have full support to achieve the goals of the organization. If you are engaged in the process, this will be a very supportive and professionally stimulating place to work. But if you are disengaged, if you do not tell your leader in a timely manner about barriers that inhibit your goal achievement, or if you only have excuses for lack of performance, then this job or organization is probably not the best match for you."

The role of the leaders is to create an environment for success rather than one that is enabling and co-dependent. This is accountability in action. If our actions as leaders do not connect with the ultimate goals and visions of our organizations, then accountability issues will erode the foundation of our work. Accountability is not just about one person doing the right thing or taking action; it is about all of us creating a culture of accountability. A culture of accountability involves building systems and communication structures that support consistent action. It also includes reflective communication among groups of leaders, as well as well-thought-out systems of checks and balances that support this reflection.

> *The role of the leaders is to create an environment for success rather than one that is enabling and co-dependent.*

SECTION A

Answers to the Most Frequently Asked Questions about Competency Assessment

Regulations and Standards

Many of our beginning discussions around competency assessment start with a question: "What do the regulations and standards say we have to do about competency assessment?"

There are several regulatory bodies that have standards for competency assessment. These regulatory groups include The Joint Commission, DNV, Centers for Medicare and Medicaid Services (CMS), federal and state agencies, and associations that oversee professional practice and standards (i.e. radiation medicine, perioperative nursing, American Heart Association CPR certification, etc.). Many of these regulatory bodies have standards that address participation in some form of competency assessment. What these regulatory bodies do not contain in their standards are detailed lists of competencies that we must measure, nor do they prescribe ways in which we must do competency assessment. Most regulatory bodies state that we need to "engage in some form of competency assessment." Our goal is to define competency assessment and then follow through on what we say we will do. The regulatory bodies don't determine what we have to measure or how we have to measure it; we do. However, once we've put those determinations into writing, regulatory bodies will hold us accountable for the definitions and plans we create.

I've seen organizations across the world get "dinged" by regulatory bodies for failing to follow *policies they've created for themselves.*

Here are some common themes that are reflected in the standards of most of the regulatory bodies that discuss competency assessment:

- The organization (not the regulatory body) needs to define competency.

- The organization needs to have a plan for competency assessment.

- The organization needs to provide orientation/initial competency assessment.

- The organization needs to do some kind of periodic competency assessment.

- The organization needs to take action if a staff member does not meet expectations.

- These actions need some kind of documentation that reflects competency assessment.

The regulatory bodies point us in a basic direction, and then we create internal organizational policies to drive our specific actions. In addressing this direction in competency assessment, organizations often create many specific internal policies that become expectations and then mandatory actions. Sometimes these are necessary actions, but often they are not. It's important to assess whether our current policies are timely and relevant or whether we've just kept adding policies year after year without discarding any.

When building a strong, solid competency assessment process, it is essential to know which driving factors are coming from external standards and which are coming from internal organizational policies. We do not have much influence over external standards, but we do have influence over our internal policies. Many times people get confused by what is external and what is internal. It is very common for people to believe that every internal policy comes from an external regulatory group because for so many years they have heard these expectations described as "a standard we have to comply with." Few people ever check the true source of these so-called regulations.

> *It is essential to know which driving factors are coming from external standards and which are coming from internal organizational policies.*

Here is a typical example of a regulatory standard and potential internal policies that may complement the standard:

External Regulatory Standard

"Incorporate restraints into your periodic competency assessment process . . ."

Internal Organizational Policy, Example 1

The organization requires every individual who may potentially apply restraints in a care situation to demonstrate competency in using restraints, every year at a skills fair. This may include everyone from nurses to security officers.

Internal Organizational Policy, Example 2

The organization requires that all employees take an on-line competency test on restraints that assesses their knowledge of correct restraint use and application.

Internal Organizational Policy, Example 3

The organization requires that all departments or areas that can potentially use restraints *consider* restraints in their competency selection each year.

In this last example, since it is a high-risk item, they reflect on it each and every competency cycle. They will actually select it as a competency in their area when it is showing evidence of one of these criteria:

- It is a new aspect of practice.
- There is a change in procedure or documentation.
- It has shown itself to be a problematic aspect of the work evidence in that area.

So if, for example, there is a change in the procedure of this high-risk skill, then that year (and perhaps that year only) a department would select it as a competency. The next year this item would be reviewed again to see if it still needs to be a competency.

I'm sure it will not surprise you that the first two examples meet the standard, but it's very common for people to be surprised that Example 3 meets the external regulatory standard of "incorporating restraints into the periodic competency assessment process." What people rarely realize is that through *considering* whether to measure competency on use of restraints each year, you have "incorporated restraints into the periodic competency process" (which is all the external standard asks you to do). It is extremely common in organizations all over the world for people to make policies they aren't required to make and then to get cited by regulatory bodies for not adhering to their own self-inflicted policies.

> *It is extremely common in organizations all over the world for people to make policies they aren't required to make and then to get cited by regulatory bodies for not adhering to their own self-inflicted policies.*

There is never just one right answer to how a regulatory standard can be met. Still, there is a widespread misconception that the only way to meet a regulatory standard is to line everybody up and check off whether they can demonstrate competency related to the standard. This misconception often leads to the creation of competency assessment processes that eat up time and money with activities that don't move the organization any closer to meeting standards or providing better care.

I strongly suggest you look at the external standard directly when identifying which competencies to address in your formal competency assessment process. Then look at your internal policies and ask the question, "Does this policy serve us or control us?" Your policies should help you achieve your goal of excellent patient care, not make life more complicated.

Float Pool Competencies

Many organizations have a resource pool of staff members, or what is often called a "float pool." At the least, an organization may have a system to move staff members from one unit/department to another as needed.

Whether employees are in a designated resource/float pool position or are floated from one unit/department to another, competency issues arise. We ask, quite rightly, if this person has the skills, knowledge, and ability to function in this capacity.

A common response to this situation is to expect staff who float frequently to a certain area to demonstrate competencies specific to that area. Another common response is to provide cross-training on a regular basis for certain shared areas in hopes that this will increase the ability to share staff more efficiently and effectively.

Although these efforts provide some benefits, most of the time we hear from the staff who float and the team that receives them, "This person is (or I am) not prepared well enough to take on a typical assignment."

So what do we do? If we have a permanent float or resource pool in which individuals may potentially float to 27 different areas, are we expecting that these individuals will be able to function independently in all 27 of these areas?

I have observed the process of floating for many years. I have talked with people who float and people in the units/departments that received them. Time and again, I see and hear the problems and questions that arise. But more importantly, I am starting to see very clearly some common factors that facilitate successful floating processes. Rather than asking people about occasions in which floating seemed not to work well, I asked the opposite:

- Who was the best float nurse you ever received? What made him or her the best?

- Tell me about a time when you floated or receive a float nurse, and it turned out to be very helpful to the unit.

The themes that emerged really revealed to me the true competencies needed when floating staff to different areas. These success factors are three competencies that make a float nurse truly successful in a given area (for a day, an hour, or other time period). And guess what? These three competencies do not have a strong clinical component. I am not saying that clinical competency is not needed. I am saying that the three most relevant competencies have a different focus for success.

Top 3 floating competencies for floating staff:

1. Learning on the Fly
2. Marketing Yourself in a Positive Way
3. Understanding Crisis Management Options

I believe that these competencies also serve us well in routine practice in our own areas as well. Let's see what we can learn by looking at each of these competencies individually.

Learning on the Fly

The "learning on the fly" competency has two parts to it. First I need to know what I do not know, and be able to speak up about it.

"I have never done that before."

"I have not done that in a while."

"I am not sure about that."

"I think there are some updates on that since I last did something like it."

On the other hand, "I will take my best guess," are not the words (or attitude) of strong people who want to learn as they go. Stating what I am uncertain about takes courage, and remembering that my priority is always giving exemplary patient care can very quickly help me find that courage.

However, that is just the first step. Saying, "I don't know how to do that" is not a "get out of jail free" card. The second step in the "learning on the fly" competency is the ability to initiate my own education. These words and attitudes exemplify the second essential aspect of "learning on the fly":

"I am not sure about this procedure . . . . I am going to look it up."

"I am going to ask someone how to do this."

"I am going to call another department to check out what we should do."

"I will use the resources that are available to guide my actions."

Obviously, this does not work for every procedure and task we do, but many times the "learning on the fly" skill is used successfully when floating. For example, a nurse floats from a medical-surgical area to dialysis. The nurse has never worked in dialysis before and does not know how to do dialysis. This nurse may be successful by respectfully acknowledging the fact to the charge nurse or supervisor and asking if someone can set up the dialysis and point out the basic things to watch for when monitoring this patient on dialysis. He or she may also ask to buddy up with another professional to ask further questions to support the patient's care. The important thing is to propose ways you *can* be useful while remaining open to learning new things.

Marketing Yourself in a Positive Way

Most of the time, if I float to a temporary work area or receive a float nurse into my work area, I will hear (or say) some examples of negative ways of marketing oneself.

"I was told to come here."

"I was pulled from my area to come over here."

"I have never worked here before."

"I was never cross-trained."

"I am not that familiar or comfortable with working in this area or specialty."

"I do not know how to do any of those things."

The "marketing yourself in a positive way" competency has two components.

1. State, in a positive way, why you are there.

2. Offer yourself as a gift.

When floating to an area, I recommend making these two statements:

1. "My name is _____. I am floating to your unit for this shift. I am here to help you out."

2. "I have the following skills that I can offer to you today, and you can see how they may fit into what is needed. I can do _____, and I can do _____, and . . ." and so on.

I have seen that when nurses float to an area with the ability to market themselves in a positive way, the results are much better. The success of the shift and of the float experience do not lie in the clinical skills that are a strong match for that specialty, but instead in the "can do" attitude the person brings. When the float nurse is willing to help in any way, and is clear about what he or she is good at, those skills will fit in a very creative way.

Understanding Crisis Management Options

Most of the time when a nurse is floated to an area, that area is under stress, stretched, or moving into crisis mode because they don't have enough staff to meet the needs. They need help to function, so they reach out for support. The float nurse can provide care and/or service assistance to help the team get the routine work done, but can also offer something else: a fresh perspective or insight that the group may have trouble seeing. In our usual routines, we often rely on familiar systems and structures that help us get the work done. There may be other systems that can also work, but they are not always part of our routine, so they may be overlooked. If a float nurse has some awareness of other systems, that person can share these ideas with the team he or she is trying to help and support. An awareness and understanding of, or competency with, various care delivery options, work-sharing systems, or alternative work distribution can be very helpful to the receiving team as they strategize their success for the shift.

Here is an example:

I am an oncology/med-surg nurse. If I were asked to float to the Intensive Care Unit (ICU), I would look at the situation in the following way. I know that I am not an ICU nurse. I would not want to take an independent patient assignment because I know I do not have the ICU-specific competencies to be successful. But I know for certain that I can help this ICU team. I would begin by marketing myself in a positive way, by introducing myself and stating that I am here to help.

Then I would use my crisis management skills. I know that most ICUs and other care areas use "total patient care" as their care delivery model. In total patient care, a nurse is given an assignment of a patient or group of patients, and another nurse has another assignment. Here is what I would suggest to the ICU team or charge nurse when I float: "I am floating to you today to help you out. I suggest we use a Partners-in-Practice model. This is where you pair me with a nurse from your staff and give us a double assignment. I will do the non-ICU-specific skills of care and assessment, and the ICU nurse will focus on the

ICU-specific items. We will work together as a two-RN team, and the patient will have safe care provided by skilled individuals."

If I were to take an independent assignment and try my best to do the ICU-specific care, I may cause harm to the patient. By using another care delivery approach in the ICU with just two of the team members, we will have a better outcome for the patients and the team.

Having knowledge of many care delivery options or crisis management strategies can be a great gift that a team can utilize. For this reason, I would suggest that any permanent float pool group develop this competency of "understanding crisis management options" in all its team members. It has a direct impact on outcomes.

Various systems of care—total patient care, team nursing, functional nursing, partners-in-practice, etc.—have different ways to assign and share care. An awareness of each and insight into when to apply them, can greatly increase our success on any given shift.

This skill of understanding crisis management options can work in any area, not just nursing care units. I have seen teams in sterile processing, lab, security, and other areas rethink the service systems for the shift because they were short-staffed and/or using temporary replacements to help out. They changed the normal flow of the work temporarily to match the crisis situation and still produced their desired outcome.

Checklists vs. "Checklists"

Over the years, I have tried to get people to look beyond checklists as the primary method to verify competencies. So many people have told me, "We are drowning in checklists in our competency assessment process!"

First, let's talk about the term *checklist.* Checklists can be used in health care in two very different ways. Using checklists as a competency verification method is different from using a checklist as part of a procedure each time the procedure is performed.

One: Documenting Return Demonstration of a Procedure to Assess Competency

A checklist can be used as a return demonstration tool to watch someone perform a procedure and confirm that he or she did each step correctly and is aware of the steps for performing the procedure. This can be used quite effectively to verify technical skills: the person performs the skill competently and is checked off the list. However, this checklist-based return demonstration is only one of eleven methods of competency verification. Return demonstration is not good for assessing critical thinking skills or interpersonal skills, and in many instances there are far more efficient methods for verifying technical skills as well.

Two: Assuring Consistent, Safe Performance of Procedures in Real Time

Checklists can be used to guide our actions each time a procedure is done. For more on this use of the checklist, I'll defer to another authority.

Atul Gawande, in his book *The Checklist Manifesto* (2009), describes the importance of checklists as tools in health care. He says:

> "We have accumulated stupendous know-how. We have put it in the hands of some of the most highly trained, highly skilled, and hardworking people in

our society. And, with it, they have indeed accomplished extraordinary things. Nonetheless, that know-how is often unmanageable. Avoidable failures are common and persistent, not to mention demoralizing, and frustrating across many fields from medicine to finance, business to government. And the reason is increasingly evident: the volume and complexity of what we know has exceeded our individual ability to deliver its benefits correctly, safely and reliably. Knowledge has both saved and burdened us." (Gawande, 2009, p. 13)

Gawande offers the checklist as a solution to help us navigate this complex world. When doing a procedure, following the same set of steps each time can provide us with a measure of protection against failure and negative outcomes. Checklists, and the routines they create, instill a kind of discipline that leads to higher performance.

> *Using checklists as a competency verification method is different from using a checklist as part of a procedure each time the procedure is performed.*

In this second situation, a checklist is not used to verify someone's competence. Here checklists are tools that the professional will use each and every time a procedure is performed. A pilot will do a pre-check before a flight using a checklist with another professional. A nurse will use a checklist before and after surgery to monitor the patient. A pharmacist will use a checklist to prepare chemotherapeutic agents under a protective hood so as not to breathe in the vapors while mixing. Even though these checklists become very routine, they need to be followed each time. The one time they are not followed can lead to grave outcomes for ourselves and/or those we are trying to serve.

I highly recommend integrating checklists and/or having a second person check your work, as part of activities that are high-risk, low-volume, and not time-sensitive. This use of a checklist protocol, each and every time, will facilitate positive outcomes, each and every time.

Now let's get back to the idea of using checklists as a verification tool in competency assessment. I strongly encourage organizations to limit their use of this verification method as much as possible. Using a checklist for competency assessment is not wrong (unless you're assessing critical thinking or interpersonal skills); it is just overused. Some organizations use it for nearly all their competency verification. In fact, some organizations are unaware that their competency form is actually a big checklist. When your competency form has a space on each competency for a "validator" to sign, that's a signal that you really just have a big checklist.

Competent Person vs. Competent Action

We have to understand that there are some procedures that are done so infrequently, and yet are so high-risk, that we can never really accomplish the goal of having all of our people be competent in them. Instead, we have to make sure we have *competent action* happening in those scenarios whenever they occur. Even if we see a condition or procedure only twice in the next decade, we have to act competently 100% of the time. This reality requires a shift from thinking that we have to make people competent to focusing on ensuring competent action.

I believe we never really lose a skill, but we can become rusty or lose proficiency. As a nurse, over the years I got very proficient at taking blood pressure readings. I worked in a post-surgical unit taking blood pressures all day long. I could take the blood pressure reading and talk to the patient and family at the same time. It became automatic. Recently, I needed to take a blood pressure on a family member in my home. It has been more than a decade since I worked in a post-surgical unit. All these years later I knew what steps to take; I had not lost my knowledge of this skill, but my actions were far from automatic. I had to think about how to hold the cuff and place the stethoscope. When someone started to talk to me at the same time, I had to ask her to wait a moment while I did the blood pressure placement and reading. I did not have the same proficiency in my skill as I'd had before.

Now imagine being shown a procedure once or a few times but never really getting a chance to do it yourself. Or perhaps the procedure requires a skill that does not get used very often. This occurs a lot when we have skills that are high-risk and low-volume. Many emergency procedures fit this high-risk/low-volume category. An important question to ask ourselves is, "How do we make sure people are competent to do the high-risk skills that they don't get much (or any) opportunity to practice in real life?"

As we consider how to help people build and maintain competency in these crucial high-risk/low-volume skills, we divide the skills into two categories: time-sensitive and not time-sensitive.

Building and Maintaining High-Risk/Low-Volume/Time-Sensitive Skills

A high-risk/low-volume skill is time-sensitive if it needs to be done impromptu or quickly. A good example is cardiopulmonary resuscitation (CPR). This is something that most of us do not do very often in our work area, but when we need to perform it, we need to jump in right away. For these high-risk/low-volume/time-sensitive situations, I suggest presenting regular CPR classes and demonstrations, staging mock events, and practicing regularly. The whole American Heart Association program is built on the concept of periodic learning and demonstration events with certification cards and expiration dates.

All of these actions around CPR, if practiced often enough, create an automatic skill in us. Sports teams build and maintain the same type of automatic behavior with practice drills, the military does it with training and maneuvers, and airline personnel do it with simulations. These are great ways to make these high-risk/low-volume/time-sensitive actions automatic.

Building and Maintaining High-Risk/Low-Volume Skills That Are *Not* Time-Sensitive

High-risk/low-volume procedures that are not time-sensitive include activities which, if done incorrectly, may cause harm, but for which we do not need to dive into the activity within seconds or a few minutes. One example is setting up a high-risk medication in a drip that will be infused over time, something that the professionals in this area do only once or twice a year. When it needs to be done, we have 20-30 minutes to get it ready for the patient. It is not an emergency, but it is high-risk because an error could cause harm to the patient.

For these high-risk/low-volume but not time-sensitive activities, I suggest avoiding competency check-offs at a skills fair or requiring a return demonstration. These will not create a competent team for this rarely done procedure, and will be costly activities with very little return on investment. When a unit may see this event or situation only once or twice a year, it doesn't make sense to train 50-100 staff members to be fully competent to respond when it occurs. Checking everyone off once a year is not going to make a strong, competent team.

For these situations in which the procedure is not time-sensitive, I recommend incorporating the competency element right into the procedure itself. Write the procedure or protocol to include a step-by-step checklist, and include a section in which one or two other professionals check the work before proceeding.

ANSWERS TO THE MOST FREQUENTLY ASKED QUESTIONS ABOUT COMPETENCY ASSESSMENT

Here is an example:

We need to set up an insulin drip for a patient in diabetic ketoacidosis (DKA). We need to bring his glucose down slowly over the next few hours or days. Dropping the blood glucose too fast can cause brain swelling, so this activity is high-risk. We only see patients with sugars this high about twice a year in our clinical area. How do we make sure we do the right thing for each patient? Since I have about 20-30 minutes to order the infusion and the insulin pump, load it, and program it, this is not a time-sensitive situation. If I were running this unit, I would write the procedure to include a competency element. List the steps needed to set up the pump and load the insulin. Once the professional has set up the pump, another professional will check his or her work. I have now integrated a competency element right into the procedure itself. Your on-the-spot competency tool or procedure checklist is not being used to deem the *person* competent; you are using a checklist to ensure that competent *action* is taking place for that patient. With the competency element written right into the procedure, even if we only see two patients a year with this situation, we can ensure that 100% of the time, competent action will occur. Conversely, by doing the skills fair once a year and checking everyone off for a competency pertaining to this high-risk/low-volume, but not time-sensitive situation, there is really nothing in place to ensure that the patient will receive competent action later.

> *For high-risk/low-volume situations in which the procedure is not time-sensitive, I recommend incorporating the competency element right into the procedure itself.*

Avoiding "Spray and Pray": Education is Not Always the Answer

When mistakes and errors occur in our organizations, it is our obligation to analyze these problems and assess the reason or reasons they occurred. These problems have many different names: sentinel events, incidents, near misses. When these errors occur, we often form a task force or committee to examine the situation, discuss it, diagram the reasons it occurred, and so on. The action of reflecting on the events is valuable and important. Where we often get stuck in our efforts to make things better is that our typical leadership response to an isolated error is to institute a house-wide mandatory competency for everyone.

This approach of "spraying" education and/or a competency requirement on everyone throughout the organization in hopes of improving things is what I call the "spray and pray" approach. We spray the education on everyone and pray that it improves outcomes.

Most people say, "Well, education can't hurt." But I beg to differ. It can actually do a great deal of harm. If we use educational strategies to address anything other than an education deficit, we send the inappropriate and even damaging message to our employees that they are not knowledgeable enough or smart enough to carry out the work. That message, when sent too often or at inappropriate times, can create an attitude of "Who cares?" or "Why try?" If an area of the organization works hard to improve, but another area makes a mistake, applying education across the board can actually hurt our overall outcomes.

It also happens often that our broadly applied efforts to improve the skills in which a few people are falling short can make the people who are excelling feel unseen and unappreciated. With a spray and pray approach, the excellers have to do the mandatory activity in spite of their excellent outcomes. They start to question why they're asked to track their outcomes at all. They wonder why they try to improve and be proactive when their efforts are never really acknowledged. I have seen organizations that use too many educational responses or mandatory competencies to solve problems turn good teams into mediocre teams, which inevitably turns good organizations into mediocre organizations. The teams and groups do not see why they should try to be proactive if it is never recognized.

Of course education is valuable, but much like a hammer, it is more valuable for some things than others. Use education only when there is a clear indication that a lack of knowledge or skill was the reason for the error. When analyzing an event, make sure the analysis includes all areas of possible deficit:

- System problems
- Availability of tools
- Departmental barriers
- Communication barriers
- Attitudinal issues
- Individual performance patterns
- Any other barriers that hinder people from taking the right actions

Here are two things that will help every educator and leader in health care to avoid falling into the trap of using the spray and pray approach:

1. First and foremost, please do a full, systematic reflection on the situation before using any education response or intervention in an effort to improve outcomes. This analysis is well worth the time and resources. Is there truly a gap in knowledge, skill, or ability? Typically there are many other contributing factors: systems issues, communication break downs, siloed department responses or support, disruptive attitudes or behaviors, issues with availability of appropriate tools or supplies, distractions in the work environment, etc.

2. When a problem is identified and thoroughly explored, do not automatically respond to that problem with an organization-wide mandatory competency. Forward the analysis to the relevant services areas and departments through the competency identification form. Seed these problematic items into the Worksheet for Identifying Ongoing Competency found on pages 25-26 of *The Ultimate Guide to Competency Assessment in Health Care*. With this approach, we are not forcing these groups or teams to *do* a competency. We are requiring them to *consider* this as a competency in light of their outcomes.

   This means that even though a mistake happens in another area, our group or team will be asked to consider and reflect on this item as a possible competency for our area. Our team will be given the outcomes and objectives that are desired in this procedure or action, and asked to reflect on our own outcomes in this area. If we are achieving the desired outcome, we do not need to consider a competency. However, if we show problems in this area or don't have enough data to be certain what our outcomes may be, we need to consider this as one of our competencies for this time period.

This approach will help move us away from the spray and pray approach and get us to a place where high performance is recognized and lower performance is addressed, but only in the areas that need it. This will save time and money while contributing to an environment that focuses on and rewards excellence. We also put ownership into the hands of the people who do the work every day, guided by the leadership vision for the whole organization.

What Every Educator and Professional Development Specialist Needs to Know

One of the major traps we get into as educators is that we often get into *doing* education, instead of *guiding* education. We need to know the difference between determining whether education is the right intervention and just doing education when someone tells us it needs to be done. If a committee of managers says we need to do house-wide education to address a problem, we as educators usually do not question it; we just carry it out, even if we do not agree with the assessment that education is the right response to a problem. For example, let's say our nosocomial infection rates are way up and quality improvement monitors show that people are not washing their hands. A committee gets together and decides we need hand washing inservices for everyone. However, it's highly doubtful that a lack of hand washing is due to a cognitive deficit in our employees. I'll bet every person knows how to wash his or her hands, and why. It is more likely that other issues are getting in the way of the person's success—things like being too busy to think, feeling overwhelmed, or not caring about outcomes or routine successes due to overall complacency. Doing hand washing inservices is not going to address these issues.

What can we do to change this? As educators, we need to remember our role as the organization's educational experts. We need to strive to feel comfortable in gently challenging any and all educational assessments that anyone in the organization is doing. It is our duty.

Here are some ways to do that:

- When you are asked to carry out an educational strategy, ask the person or group, "What is your desired outcome in this situation?" Start redirecting the conversation back to checking whether the educational strategy is the best response to the problem. Take some time to come up with other strategies to bring back to the group, each with projected outcomes and costs, so the person or group can see the appropriate application of each of the strategies.

- Educate yourself about other strategies for responding to problems and issues. Become familiar with quality/performance improvement techniques, organizational development strategies, and leadership compliance and disciplinary tactics. Being familiar with these different strategies can help you help others select the best approach.

- When a quality improvement (QI) activity has identified a problem in your organization, rather than jumping on the problem to find a solution right away, try a second level QI monitor. Dig a little deeper to discover the real problem underneath the problem identified. The hand washing illustration above is a good example. A second QI monitor can include questions like, "Who, if anyone, is doing hand washing correctly?" This can help us understand what is making the difference between failure and success, and what is getting in the way of a positive outcome.

> *Your organization needs your expertise to know when to use education and when not to use it.*

Remember, you are the educational expert! I know that some days you do not feel that way, but you are, and your organization is paying you to carry out that role. Embrace it. Your organization needs your expertise to know when to use education and when *not* to use it.

Validators

Often when competency processes are discussed and revised, the discussion turns to the question of who will be the "validator" of the competencies of an employee. How many validators do we need? How will we know the validators are competent? What kind of preparation do they need?

Let's take a nice long pause here before moving forward . . .

The assumption that we have to use validators for every competency takes us down a path that can be ominous, ineffective, and costly. When designing a competency assessment process, we need to check our assumptions about this whole concept of "validators."

Most often the term validator means that a person (manager, educator, preceptor, or other designated person) watches me perform or do my work, and determines that I am knowledgeable or competent.

Do not fall into the trap of thinking that all competencies need a validator.

Here are the most common assumptions that people have about validators. Some I have marked TRUE and some I have marked FALSE.

1. One person who is really good at the job can check off another person entering the job on all the aspects of doing the job.
   FALSE

Do not confuse the validator role with the role of the preceptor. Precepting is great. It is beneficial to have multiple points of evaluation during precepting and orientation.

However, one person cannot check me off for my whole job. One person may be very expert at one set of skills, while another person may be very expert at another set of skills, so having multiple people in the verification process is healthy when confirming a variety of competencies. It's also important to remember that the whole idea of "checking off" a competency is suitable only for technical procedures.

2. The boss knows the job as well as or better than the employee.
   FALSE

The boss/manager makes sure that the employee can fulfill the requirements of the job but is not necessarily in a position to do the job as well as the employee. In most cases they cannot. Their job is to hold employees accountable to achieve the desired outcomes. Therefore, having the boss as validator is not necessarily a good strategy; managers are usually not the best validators. If it were true that the boss knows the job as well as or better than the employee, that would mean that my boss knows how to do my job fully, and that my boss's boss would also know the job. This assumption would go all the way up to the CEO or president of the organization, who would have to know how to do the job of every person in the organization. It's just not the case, so it's important to let go of the erroneous idea that managers are our best choice for validators. Managers hold us accountable for participating in competency assessment processes.

3. Validators can be utilized to verify technical skills for which a return demonstration is selected as the verification method.
   TRUE

The best time to use a validator (or validators) in competency assessment is with a return demonstration, which is a good option for measuring technical skills. Remember, however, that a return demonstration is not good for measuring critical thinking skills or interpersonal skills. There are other more appropriate methods to measure critical thinking and interpersonal skills (Wright 2005, Chapter 4, Competency Assessment Verification Methods). Again, do not fall into the trap of thinking that all competencies need a validator. Watching or observing someone do something is an approach we can use for procedures and other technical skills, but it will not achieve the goals for assessing other competencies.

Reflection on the Concept of Validators

If you take only one thing away from this section, let it be that when you start to think about verifying competencies, do not immediately think you need a validator. A validator is useful when using a return demonstration in a skills fair, simulation, or in practice to observe the ability to perform a technical skill. But do not think that a validator is put in place to measure all of your competencies. This is just not possible.

> *When you start to think about verifying competencies, do not immediately think you need a validator.*

So the question that often arises is, "Since the manager is ultimately accountable for competency assessment of

ANSWERS TO THE MOST FREQUENTLY ASKED QUESTIONS ABOUT COMPETENCY ASSESSMENT

employees, but the manager's role is not to be the validator, what is the manager's role in competency assessment?"

While the manager is accountable to ensure that an employee is competent to do a given job, it's the manager's job to put a system in place to make this happen rather than to do it. The manager then confirms by a (possibly annual) signature that this process has been completed to show that the employee is competent to continue in this role. That signature does not mean that the manager watched the person do all kinds of competencies. The manager's final documentation means that the employee has collected data (through self-actions or with others) to confirm his or her current identified competencies.

Here is an example:

We want to make sure that the Clinical Nurse Specialist (CNS) for Med-Surg is competent in inserting PICC lines. I am this person's manager. I do not know how to insert PICC lines, but I am accountable to make sure this person is doing things competently. In order to make sure this happens, some or all of these data points may be collected to confirm this person's competence:

- A completed certificate from the PICC line company that the CNS completed the PICC insertion class given by the vendor's instructor.

- Placement x-rays or images that indicated correct placement. These are often done for patient safety and placed in the patient record. After removing the personal patient information, this data can be used to verify competency.

- Infection control records that show the outcomes of the first 10 PICC lines inserted by this CNS. This quality data is often automatically collected on these lines. The employee gathers this data and brings it forward to the manager (or submits it through another designated record-keeping process).

We may only have one person in the organization who can insert a PICC line, so this is how we confirm that the person is competent in the technical skill of PICC insertion. In this case, no validator is needed—just a strong competency assessment process that utilizes our data and outcomes.

In summary, validators can be used to validate some technical skills, but validators are not the core of your competency process. We should not make them the center of validation for a group's competencies. If we do, we take ownership, empowerment, and accountability away from our staff. If we put the employee at the center of the verification process, we will be much happier with the overall outcomes of our competency process.

Competencies Can be Used as the Second Half of the Job Description

Competency assessment is not just for assessing skills. It can also be used as a way to articulate the current requirements of a job. In essence, it can be the second half of the job description.

Here is how to do it:

Competency assessment should reflect the current competencies needed in the job. It is not a static list of skills repeated over and over again each year. It is a dynamic list that reflects what is new, changing, high-risk, and/or problematic (Wright, 2005). A dynamic competency identification process can help us create a list of competencies that will reflect the current nature of the job by featuring the technologies, knowledge, and concepts needed to complete the work competently.

When we have a dynamic system in place for competency assessment, we also have achieved another aspect of performance management: articulating expectations. By stating what has changed in the job, we are explaining to employees some very specific aspects of where their performance now needs to be. Our jobs are constantly changing, and competency assessment can help leaders articulate these changes.

So now, competency assessment becomes part of the job description. If we think about it, the traditional job description is the basic part of the job that does not change much: "Do your job, come to work on time, be able to lift 25 pounds, etc." The second half of the job description should be current competencies. This will reflect the part of the job that changes, and more importantly, it will put relevant information about what is expected from the team right in front of them. In a way we are saying to the employees, "Now your job looks like this: you now need to learn how to use this piece of equipment, here is some new research that needs to be integrated into our work, and here is an area where we need to improve our outcomes by changing our practices in this way."

Now, when someone asks if they can see the current job description for this job, we can show them two documents: the traditional job description and this year's identified competencies. Then next year, if someone asks us the same thing, we can produce the traditional job description as well as that year's revised set of identified competencies. By using a dynamic competency identification process, we are automatically updating our job descriptions every year. We have created a wonderful performance management system that assesses competencies and articulates expectations at the same time.

Performance Review and Competency Assessment: How Do they Fit Together?

Performance appraisal and competency assessment fall into the same basic category: the employee evaluation process. But they also have some differences. Performance appraisal often refers to evaluation of the employee's overall performance. Competency assessment is the component of a performance appraisal that evaluates the current competencies required for the job. Performance appraisal and competency assessment may or may not be linked in the same tracking system (paper or automated), but they are both part of the employee evaluation process.

Here are a few basic guidelines for handling the timing of each evaluation system:

- Performance appraisal can be done on a **cyclical basis** (an annual date), in which all employees get their performance appraisals at the same time, or it can be done on a **staggered basis**, in which employees are reviewed on their anniversary date. (More on this can be found on pages 173-176 of *The Ultimate Guide to Competency Assessment in Health Care*.)

    Some organizations do performance appraisals on the anniversary of hire for each employee. Other organizations select a date on which all employees will have their performance appraisals. The overall purpose of performance appraisal time is to have a formal opportunity for supervisor and employee to have a discussion. During this time, the supervisor and employee review the individual's overall performance for the year, and set goals for the next year. This meeting is NOT the only time we evaluate the employee. That is actually being done throughout the year. If there is a performance issue on any day of work, a supervisor will address it at the time rather than waiting months to bring up the issue.

- Competency assessment should *only* be done on a **cyclical** basis, in which everyone starts and ends at the same time. Do not use the employee's anniversary date for competency assessment.

    Use either a designated annual date or a shorter cycle, e.g. "Everyone has to have this competency done by the end of the month." Just be sure that everyone has the same amount of time to complete the competency. Competency assessment reflects the ever-changing nature of the job, so competency assessment communicates the latest expectations for the skills required for the job functions. Therefore each employee needs to have the same amount of time to accomplish this development or advancement of the new requirements or changes in knowledge or skill. If we used anniversary dates, employees would have different time frames within which to complete the required competencies. Legally, that would be viewed as not providing employees with equal opportunities.

    For example, if one of the new competencies for this year is that all employees of a certain job category need to know how to operate a new piece of equipment, each employee must learn how to use it and verify competency in its use. If we use anniversary dates, some employees may only have a few weeks to attain and show competence, while other employees might have as long as eleven months. Therefore we would have different expectations for employees in the same job category. That would be viewed as an unfair employment practice and should be avoided.

An initial aspect of competency assessment is articulating what is new and/or changing in the job. A subsequent aspect is verifying those expectations. By doing competency assessment on a cyclical basis, every employee is given the same time to complete the competency assessment.

Competency assessment and performance appraisal can be done together as one system, or they can each be done as two separate systems or tracking processes. Either is okay; we just need to know the purpose and rationale our organization has for each and how we will use this information in overall employee evaluation. This will help keep our system strong and healthy for all employees and the organization.

> *In competency assessment, everyone starts and ends at the same time. Do not use the employee's anniversary date for competency assessment.*

Standardization vs. Sameness

A common request I hear from organizations and health systems is that they want to "standardize" their competencies and competency process. Sometimes their first step in trying to achieve this is to develop a core set of competencies that everyone does. However, having everyone do the same competencies does not necessarily standardize the process. I think organizations do this hoping that the process will move everyone to the same level of excellence.

So how can we achieve standardization without trying to make everything exactly the same? How can we allow each group to reflect their unique personalities and needs, and still keep the whole organization moving in the same direction?

Standardization focuses on the goal. For example, we often create standardized guidelines for the procedure to achieve the desired outcomes, but the actual procedure may require different steps in various settings—operating rooms, ambulatory surgery centers, emergency departments, oncology units, clinics—because the equipment, space, and customer needs will vary. If we tried to make everything the same it would not work.

Organizations need policies, procedures, and guidelines. We need to articulate the outcomes we want to achieve and identify the systems that are in place to achieve those outcomes. Then we need to have measurements in place to make sure these goals are met. These measurement efforts include quality monitoring, evaluations, and outcomes tracking. Standardization can include a set of "non-negotiable" practices that get to an outcome without having to make every policy, procedure, and guideline exactly the same for everyone.

Competencies should follow standardized policies/procedures. Competencies should be selected and verified when there is a gap identified in outcomes or when a practice changes. Doing the same basic competencies every year is not required. Holding people to the "standard" of practice is! So we continuously monitor our goals and outcomes, rather than just checking people off each year and hoping that our outcomes are therefore being met.

Do you see the strong link to quality improvement here?

Automating Our Competency Process: Tracking, Documentation, and Communication

What Kind of Competency Data do We Need to Keep?

Data that we collect on competency assessment needs to be stored, accessible, and tracked, for three clear purposes:

1. Data must be accessible to people who will be assigning work (team leaders, shift supervisors, charge nurses, etc.). They do not need to have access to the whole employee file, just to information about an employee's completed competencies so that they can make appropriate work assignments.

2. Data must be accessible to the manager at the point of service, to follow up on any deficits in an employee's performance.

3. Data must be aggregated and sent to the organizational governing body (executive team and/or board of trustees) to give them a clear picture of the current state of the organization.

Should We Track Competencies on Paper or Use an Automated System?

Competency assessment can be tracked on paper or with electronic systems. Computerized processes have the advantage of being able to search data in many more ways.

When moving to a computerized system, we need to dream first about what we want on paper, and *then* find or adapt an electronic system to make that dream a reality. Many organizations live with a system that makes them feel like they are serving the system, rather than the system serving them.

There are many tracking systems available, and there are new ones being created all the time. These are often called "talent management products," and they present a wide range of tools that support tracking of educational offerings, competency assessment, and performance appraisal information. They can also be used to:

- Track or search employee skills; for example, "Do any of our employees speak Russian?"

- Help with employee development; for example, has an employee completed orientation to a job, a piece of equipment, or a specialty area?

- Track employment history: this may include interview schedules, criminal background checks, compensation changes, re-hire eligibility, etc.

When shopping for talent management products or considering an upgrade of your current methods, here are a few things to keep in mind.

What Kind of Information or Actions Do We Want the System to Produce?

Putting information into a system is pointless unless it enables us to use the data for some purpose, so before we shop for talent management products, it's important to reflect on exactly what it is that we want those products to achieve. Most systems can and should achieve multiple goals for us.

The first step in selecting the right talent management product is to think of all the things we could possibly want from the system. Brainstorm with a group of colleagues to create a comprehensive vision for what we want this system to achieve for our organization. If your discussion generates additional questions, be sure to capture exactly what questions need to be answered.

The first step in selecting the right talent management product is to think of all the things we could possibly want from the system. Dream first. Shop second.

Warning: Do not first look at systems and see what they can do and only *then* begin to formulate a vision for what you want. If you do it this way, you will limit yourself and your organization. Most systems have a lot of potential. They can do a lot for you and can be customized to achieve many goals. Dream first. Shop second.

Who Uses the Talent Management System?

One of the most important factors to consider when choosing a talent management system is exactly who will input and track information in the system? There are three choices:

- If the manager enters and tracks the data, most of the time we have manager-centered competency assessment, education, or performance evaluation.

- If the educator is the main person tracking and watching data, then the educator takes on the major accountability for outcomes and practice.

- If the employee is the one who enters and tracks the data, then we have employee-centered ownership of their work and outcomes.

Most health care systems have a combination of all three, making it even more important to watch who is at the center of most of the entry and tracking. In the end, the talent management product will actually define major accountability philosophies for your organization. Most people don't realize this, but it's true. The tracking systems you choose will have a major impact on the articulated philosophies you have around accountability for your organization.

> *The tracking systems you choose have a major impact on the articulated philosophies you have around accountability for your organization.*

The bottom line is this: Talent management systems are only as good as the people behind them. These systems cannot perform the role of leadership for us. They cannot replace accountability for practice and outcomes. They only serve as tools to see a clearer picture of where we are and where we want to go with the very talented pool of professionals we have in our organization.

Competency and Engagement

When we do competency assessment in any form, we have the ability to uncover two kinds of performance deficits in an employee. You can uncover competency issues and you can uncover engagement (or commitment) issues. These problems are very different and require very different responses. A successful employee is one who is both competent and engaged.

Let's examine both of these components.

Being Competent

As I presented in a diagram on page 7, competency is an ever-changing target. An employee needs to come to an organization with the competencies/skills necessary to start in his or her job (or a willingness to gain these skills quickly in orientation). Then those competencies will change over time. As the organization grows and evolves, employees' competencies need to evolve as well.

Each competency cycle, we need to make sure the employees in each job category have the current competencies to be successful in their role. Competency assessment therefore is dynamic and ever-changing. It reflects new research in the field, new equipment we will now be using, changes in practice or procedures, and any areas that have been problematic in our quest to achieve our outcome goals. Therefore, if an employee says, "I have been here for 20 years. Don't you know I am competent by now?" I would respond, "The job requirements are constantly changing as the world of health care changes. If you are still using the technology, knowledge, or processes from even five years ago, you are out of date."

Being Engaged

Engagement is all about moving in the same direction as the organization. This means sharing in the vision, mission, and goals of the organization. See **Figure A.1** on the following page.

COMPETENCY ASSESSMENT FIELD GUIDE

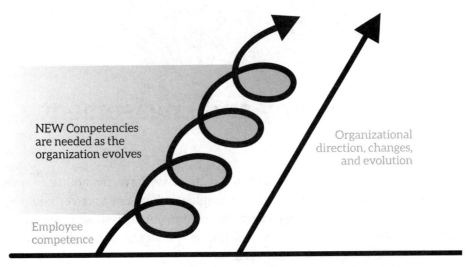

Figure A.1: Competency Evolution and Organizational Evolution

In the diagram above, the employee's movement (the spiral figure) is in the same direction as the organization evolution (the straight line).

An employee who is engaged is someone who is:

- Focused on organizational success

- Willing to adapt daily work to reach the organizational goals

At some point an employee may go off in another direction. See **Figure A.2** below.

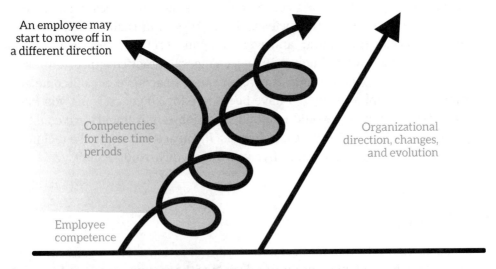

Figure A.2: Employee Deviation from Competency Evolution and Organizational Evolution

It will happen. When it does, we need to tell that person that he or she needs to come back in line with the organizational goals and direction. In other words, we need to articulate our expectations for the role or re-articulate them if we have articulated them before. (This is the free Human Resources tip of the day.)

If the employee, after being given additional clarification of expectations, refuses to come back in line—as demonstrated through his or her words and/or actions—it is best to break the contractual agreement with this individual. If we leave the person in place who clearly does not want to support the mission and goals of the group, this individual can become a toxic element to the team and the whole organization. It is very dangerous to keep them if they do not want to move in the same direction as the organization. This is an engagement issue. This person does not want to be a part of what we are all trying to do together.

Now here is the bigger point: Please do not spend a dime on educating this person. This is not an education problem. No amount of education is going to fix an engagement issue.

What to Do When We Uncover a Competency Issue

When employees are having trouble moving from one set of competencies up to another, the problem is typically about evolving their skills to include things like learning how to use new computer documentation or software, or applying new research, or operating a new piece of equipment.

In this situation, education and professional development are wonderful options. This person wants to move in the direction of the organizational goals, but is just having trouble moving from one competency level to the next, and needs a bit more support.

What to Do When We Uncover an Engagement/Commitment Issue

This is when employees refuse to participate, or they constantly have excuses for why they cannot perform, but they take no action to seek help or even communicate. They wait for deadlines to pass and then explain why they can't do something. They are burned out, bitter, or angry, and they don't really want to work in our organization (or maybe anywhere) anymore, or maybe never did. This is an engagement issue.

This situation needs to be addressed with a managerial response. The manager needs to sit down with this person and ask one basic question: "Do you really want to work here? Because your behavior is demonstrating that you do not."

Again, in this situation of lack of engagement, please do not use education or remediation. Education and remediation have become almost an automatic response from most managers and human resource professionals. By automatically applying an educational fix, we may confuse the problem and actually cover up the issue for a time, which may cause harm to a patient and negative outcomes in the organization. We need to be aware of this and use this information to guide our choices.

A Great Solution for Distinguishing Between these Two Issues

In the overview of my model (see page 6), I point out three elements for competency assessment success: ownership, empowerment, and accountability. The middle one—empowerment—asks us to put the employee at the center of competency verification. Once the competencies are selected, it becomes the responsibility of each employee to bring evidence of competence in that area. They don't just get to bring any old piece of evidence they want; it must be an approved verification method determined by the educator or council or team. The reason this is such a good solution for distinguishing between those with competency issues and those who are disengaged is that the action of bringing forward verification of competency (or the failure to do so) will clearly show either engagement or lack of it. The role of leaders is to frequently remind employees of their role in this competency process, and that if they are having any problems, they need to bring that information to the manager or educator so that he or she can get the barriers out of the way.

> *The action of bringing forward verification of competency (or the failure to do so) will very clearly show either engagement or lack of it.*

This is a nice clear way to measure engagement. It makes a clear distinction between those individuals who want to move in the direction of the organization, but are having trouble achieving the competency, and those individuals who just do not try or even care—those who are disengaged.

I recommend making sure that your policies reflect this discussion. State very clearly in your employment policies that there are two deficits that may be

ANSWERS TO THE MOST FREQUENTLY ASKED QUESTIONS ABOUT COMPETENCY ASSESSMENT

uncovered in the competency assessment process—those related to competency and those related to engagement. Both competency and engagement are required for successful employment. Also state how you will respond to each type of deficit. All competency issues will be dealt with equally and fairly according to an appropriate set of guidelines, and all engagement issues will be dealt with equally and fairly by [insert procedure language]. It's vital to be clear with everyone that people with competency issues and people with engagement issues will not all be treated the same. This makes for a much healthier organization that is based on ownership, empowerment, and accountability.

SECTION B

Reflections from Organizations that have Used the Wright Competency Model

Introduction

All over the world, as explorers and pioneers have discovered new lands and the routes to get there, they have shared and reflected on their experiences, both good and bad. They knew others would follow, and they wanted those people to travel safer, better, and farther than they did.

The first part of Section B is a collection of experiences that competency assessment explorers and pioneers have had using the Wright Competency Assessment Model. These stories come from small and large hospitals, some in big cities and some in rural settings. Some are teaching/research centers, some are government entities, and some are privately run. The stories have been selected and organized to provide the best effect for those reading through this entire section. While it may be tempting to skip stories from organizations or departments that seem unlike your own, I can assure you that the problems, pitfalls, joys, and successes of competency assessment are pretty universal. It's highly possible that someone in an organization or department that is very different from your own came up with a brilliant innovation that could save you a whole lot of time, money, and frustration!

In each story, we have lifted up the core aspects of their journey and discoveries. We have tried to capture the motivation for the journey and the realities along the path. You can see clearly what each organization or department was dealing with as its starting point and how culture, issues, and assets shaped the journey.

The second part of Section B shares a number of journeys from organizations that have achieved measurable outcomes working with the Wright Competency Model. They have made stellar gains in terms of culture, cost savings, and employee engagement.

We thank each and every organization for their contribution, and we especially want to recognize the amazing people who have so boldly led their teams into the new, uncharted land of a competency assessment process that is highly developmental and truly inspiring. Some of the paths were bumpy, but their amazing tenacity and persistence brought some wonderful, sustainable results.

Enjoy the reflections!

Stories from the Field

A Journey to Competency Brings a Culture Change

Waterbury Hospital
Waterbury, Connecticut

This community and teaching hospital understood that a well-written, comprehensive job description is the foundation of any competency/performance assessment of potential employees and new hires, as well as supporting all staff in bringing forward ongoing evidence of their skills.

Motivation for Changing Our Competency Assessment Process

At Waterbury Hospital, we have embarked on a journey—a journey to competency. It's a little like planning a trip to a brand new destination: We knew where we wanted to go, but we didn't know how to get there! The Wright Model of Competency Assessment is the "GPS" that we are using to guide us on this adventure. As we travel, we will make stops along the way, and we anticipate that there will be times when we have to recalculate our route. We will, however, reach our final destination. Our goal is to live Our Promise and keep patients at the center of everything we do. We strive to provide compassionate, high-quality, safe patient care. This outcome aligns with our vision and mission and ultimately drives our day-to-day work. That is the whole reason for our journey.

Where We Were and Where We Wanted to Go

We started our journey with a commitment from our senior leadership team to move ahead with this competency project. It was essential to have buy-in from the top down. Our leaders encouraged us to move in the direction of a competency assessment process focused on outcomes and accountability.

The first challenge we met was to help our managers and staff understand the true meaning of competency. We kicked off our project by inviting Donna Wright to consult with our Human Resources and education staff. She also presented an overview of her Model of Competency Assessment to our managers and staff. The starting point for all of us was to understand the process, including the roles of the manager, the employee, and the educator. She also helped us understand the significance of accountability in a competency assessment program. It was important for us to understand the inefficiency of our "spray and pray" solution to many employee issues in the past.

What Key Stakeholders Most Appreciated about the Model

Donna was able to excite our leaders and staff and get the momentum going. We started to incorporate her ideas into our everyday work. For the first time, the Education team did not select the competencies to be assessed in the upcoming nursing skills fair. Following Wright's Competency Assessment Model, we asked managers to work collaboratively with their staffs in identifying the most relevant topics to address. Worksheets were designed to help them note processes that were new, changing, high-risk, or problematic. Based on the information that was collected, new learning stations with meaningful competencies were incorporated into the skills fair. Staff participation was higher than previous years, and feedback was overwhelmingly positive. After this event, it was clear to us that when we empower staff by allowing them to help identify their own competencies, they become much more engaged!

Overcoming Our Most Difficult Competency Hurdles

It could be said that competency assessment starts before we hire, as potential candidates must have certain skills, knowledge, education, and/or previous experience. New hires also have initial onboarding competency assessment, with skills, knowledge, and abilities that must be validated during their orientation period. Ongoing competency assessment is done on a regular basis. The job description is the foundation of all these competency assessments and was the next challenge on our journey. We had to make sure we had job descriptions in place for all roles at our organization. Many job descriptions had to be written or updated.

REFLECTIONS FROM ORGANIZATIONS THAT HAVE USED THE WRIGHT COMPETENCY MODEL

Our Human Resources team, working with a group of educators, standardized the format and content of our job descriptions. We recognized that a well-written, comprehensive job description is the foundation of any competency/performance assessment. We made sure that all job descriptions contained job requirements (education, licenses, work experience, skills) and essential functions. We also did something we had never done before: We provided staff and their managers with copies of their job descriptions! It sounds simple, but this was a key step in building our competency program. Many staff members, especially our long-term employees, had never seen their job descriptions. They now have 24/7 online access to job descriptions, which are stored in a web-based competency assessment tool.

> *Competency assessment starts before we hire, as potential candidates must have certain skills, knowledge, education, and/or previous experience.*

The next step we undertook in our journey was to redesign our performance review process and include competency assessment in this revised tool. After consultation with Donna Wright, we redesigned our performance assessments to include her four elements of overall employee evaluation: 1) standards of performance, 2) competency assessment, 3) job requirements, and 4) an optional recognition section. Job descriptions were attached to every performance evaluation, and managers were asked to rate employees in the competency section on topics that were new, changing, high risk, or problematic. In a recent Joint Commission site visit, managers were specifically asked how those competencies were defined. Thanks to the fact that we took the time early in our project to help managers truly understand competency, they were able to respond appropriately, to the satisfaction of the site surveyor.

At this point, we are only halfway through our journey. We now have job descriptions and performance assessments in place. So, where are we heading next? Now that we have a better understanding of competency assessment and have initiated an organizational-wide culture change, we are ready to tackle a complete revision of our onboarding assessments. We have some huge challenges ahead of us. For example, we anticipate that we will meet resistance when we take away those 15-page orientation checklists and replace them with a dozen or so well written competency statements with corresponding behavioral criteria. We plan to once again consult with Donna Wright and have her guide us through this process.

Benefits to Individuals and the Organization

As we devise our own competency process here at Waterbury Hospital, we have found that it is essential to manage the whole process electronically. We are currently using a web-based tool that is easily configurable to our needs. Each hospital's tools will be unique, but the main message is that you should create your timeline and identify the tasks that you need to complete. Once you identify those project tasks, plot them out in a master document where progress can be tracked along the way. Date it. Color-code it! Do whatever it takes to make it meaningful to your project team. This is particularly helpful if you have multiple people working on the project simultaneously. We found that by putting the master project document on a shared drive, all team members could easily access the information and view and record their project progress. It worked well, and we are using the same approach as we start to work on additional initiatives this year.

> *Our leaders can now manage people, not paperwork!*

Online assessments have proven much more effective than our previous paper systems. At the present time, parts of our process (competencies) are still on paper, but we plan to continue to move everything online. This will allow us to track progress and outcomes with flexible reporting, and there will never be another lost or incomplete onboarding assessment. Our leaders can now manage people, not paperwork!

As we move along on our journey, we continue to find detours along the way, but because we are absolutely clear about where we want to go, we simply follow an alternate route. We are also finding that our journey is taking us longer than anticipated. Instilling a change in mindset and getting people to think of competency assessment in a totally different way will take several years to implement. However, we are satisfied that we are heading in the right direction. The signs are clear that our organization's collaborative process to establish effective competency management will ultimately result in a culture of patient safety, quality care, and staff empowerment.

Susan Regan O'Brien, MS, BS
Education Consultant
Education Department
Waterbury Hospital

Competency as the Key to a Nursing Practice Model

Lawrence Memorial Hospital
Lawrence, Kansas

This community-owned hospital embraced Relationship-Based Care, using the Wright Competency Model as the key to developing and enculturating a model for nursing practice.

Motivation for Changing Our Competency Assessment Process

What drove the change in our competency process was different at different levels of our organization. Many times it is frustration over a current process that drives the search for a better way. I will always remember the morning when our vice president of nursing came into my office with Donna Wright's book in her hand. She was new to her role but not new to our hospital. She had begun to lead the initiation of something we had never had before: a model for nursing practice. The model was Relationship-Based Care (RBC). With the bright green book, *The Ultimate Guide to Competency Assessment*, in her hand, she asked if I had ever heard of this framework. I pulled my copy out of my drawer and we gave each other a nod. We were in alignment, and I knew that whatever we created together was going to be good. She asked how I felt about implementing this model, and I replied that I had been ready for quite some time. I was frustrated with our current method of competency assessment and had tried to implement Donna's model several times without success.

Even as a new senior leader, our vice president of nursing understood that the education team would be key in implementing all the changes she wanted to lead. She asked me to charter our first house-wide shared leadership council—the Education Council. We agreed that the council should be interdisciplinary with a collaborative approach. Our first vice-chair of the council was a respiratory therapist. The initial purpose of the Education Council was to lead the implementation of the Wright Competency Model and to provide education leadership for the entire RBC implementation and shared leadership initiative. The stars were in alignment and we were ready to begin.

Where We Were and Where We Wanted to Go

As I said, previous attempts to change our competency assessment were unsuccessful. Resistance to changing our current process, a marathon skills fair, was strong because a lot of staff could complete the process in a short time. As a Staff Development Specialist, I knew that our current process had very little meaning in growing our staff. Like many hospitals, we held house-wide and department-specific skills fairs; ours consisted of approximately 20 stations that all clinical licensed staff completed over a four-day period. Some staff members rushed through as fast as they could, some grumbled, and some were downright angry as they came through the marathon days of the skills fair. There was very little emphasis on improving professional practice for the provision of excellent patient care. Staff were frustrated because the process meant little other than a hurdle to jump over in order to keep their jobs.

> *We knew that competency development had a direct impact not only on patient outcomes but on the empowerment of our staff.*

Our dream was for staff to lead their own competency development process, to be engaged in their own professional growth. We knew that competency development had a direct impact not only on patient outcomes but on the empowerment of our staff.

What Key Stakeholders Most Appreciated about the Model

Initially some staff members were confused, feeling that the process was too easy (instead of 20 competencies, there were now 5). But many staff members shared that, for the first time, the competencies made sense to them and helped them in their practice. A staff member who had just moved into a new role said about our competency assessment model, "It legitimized my new role."

REFLECTIONS FROM ORGANIZATIONS THAT HAVE USED THE WRIGHT COMPETENCY MODEL

Directors like the empowerment that the model gives their staff and appreciate that our organization now has a common understanding of what competencies are. They appreciate the identification worksheet (the Worksheet for Identifying Ongoing Competencies found in *The Ultimate Guide to Competency Assessment in Health Care* on pages 25-26), especially the utilization of performance improvement data for the development of competencies.

Educators value the self-directed learning and critical thinking that are integrated throughout the process.

Our vice president of nursing's vision of the value of this model in bringing change to our organization was essential to our success. I asked her what she thought of the implementation of the model and she said, "Staff see the value in competency assessment."

Overcoming Our Most Difficult Competency Hurdles

Change is difficult. It is hard to embrace new ways of doing things when we have done them a certain way for so long. People change at different rates. For some people the model is easy to understand; for others it is more difficult to embrace. The understanding of the model was not role-specific but more person-specific. This is a dynamic process—new leadership, new staff, and/or new educators can create challenges.

Benefits to Individuals and the Organization

Our new competency process has helped create an environment of meaningful growth and change, developing a more confident, empowered staff that is better equipped to care for their patients, each other, and themselves.

Rose Schaffer, MS, RN
Staff Development Specialist
Lawrence Memorial Hospital

From Fragmentation to Consistency and Alignment

Buena Vista Regional Medical Center
Storm Lake, Iowa

This regional medical center transformed a fragmented, inconsistent unit-based competency system into a systematic, hospital-wide assessment of competencies that are aligned with organizational and departmental goals.

Motivation for Changing Our Competency Assessment Process

Our competency process was disjointed and inconsistent. We lacked an organization-wide competency assessment process. Each department had its own system for assessing staff competency; some nonclinical departments felt that competency assessment did not apply to them.

Where We Were and Where We Wanted to Go

Most of the clinical departments had competency checklists which were completed by each employee checking himself or herself off or being checked off by a peer. The checklist contained the same items every year, and the results were not used in employee performance evaluations. Our process provided no meaning for staff or their leaders.

Our dream was to have a uniform, systematic, meaningful competency process that would apply to people in all positions (staff and leaders), hardwired for initial and ongoing competencies and aligned with our organizational and departmental goals.

We are now in the third year of implementation, having implemented with our leadership team the first year, then for staff in year two. We are now in year three and have implemented across the organization. This process is now mandatory for all job categories, with consequences for non-adherence. Our process consists of department-wide brainstorming sessions with discussions that include new/emerging technology, new processes, or any services that may trigger a need for competency validation. The brainstorming sessions are led by the department directors with assistance from a member of the competency work group (steering committee) as requested. Following the brainstorming session, specific competencies for each role/job description in the department are selected from the brainstorming list. Once the competencies are selected, competency statements are written and the validation methods are determined. Validation templates for documentation have been created for each type of validation method. These are available on a shared website and readily accessible for leaders. Then the process of validation commences! Timelines for completion are clearly defined.

Throughout this process, leaders were encouraged to integrate the competency validation process with other organizational work/initiatives. For example, the organization has established goals around improving the patient experience. Departments have established goals that support this organizational goal, so leaders are encouraged to establish department competencies around this goal as well. Our hope is to have the competency validation process support other work we are focused on.

What Key Stakeholders Most Appreciated about the Model

Our new competency process applies to everyone —staff and leaders. No one is exempt. Staff members are provided with continuous learning and find greater meaning in their jobs by being included in the brainstorming sessions to determine what competencies are most important to assess. Our competencies now align with our organizational and departmental goals.

Overcoming Our Most Difficult Competency Hurdles

Some leaders felt that their unit's current process and tool (the checklist) were sufficient. Some leaders perceived that the new model created more paperwork for them.

Some staff members found articulating the competencies in writing to be a challenge. Understanding the difference between technical skills and leadership skills was also a challenge for some. Accepting who can validate each competency was difficult for some as well.

> *Our competencies now align with our organizational and departmental goals.*

Benefits to Individuals and the Organization

We now have a systematic, hospital-wide competency process for all staff and leaders. We have established clear expectations that the competency process applies to everyone. The workgroup has standardized the validation forms so that they are user-friendly and can be used across all departments.

The first year was a trial year. We are currently on year three and completion of competency assessment is required as a condition of employment.

Michele Kelly, RN, MSN
Executive Director of Quality
Buena Vista Regional Medical Center

Maximum Staff Involvement Creates its Own Momentum

Kettering Behavioral Medical Center
Kettering, Ohio

Implementation of a specific competency for psychiatric codes led to significantly improved patient outcomes. Staff who participated in developing a validation method for the competency are now noticeably more engaged.

Motivation for Changing Our Competency Assessment Process

We saw an increase in the number of restraint episodes in 2012. Staff were responding inappropriately to the "code violets" (psychiatric emergencies with an aggressive or violent patient) we had on the unit, including calling the police, not restraining patients who were meeting criteria for restraint, and verbalizing that they were afraid.

Where We Were and Where We Wanted to Go

Responses to codes were disorganized. Staff members felt they lacked competence and confidence in dealing with aggressive patients. We needed education and assessment to help staff members develop knowledge and competence and gain confidence in successfully and safely de-escalating patient situations.

We got staff involved in the planning process by developing a fun way for them to participate. Staff created scenarios for movie clips that highlighted our current issues in an amusing way in one scenario, then filmed another that demonstrated how the code should work in the future. Staff enjoyed seeing their peers in the clips and appreciated the visual demonstration. Since implementation of the competency, restraint episodes have decreased by almost 50%, and no inappropriate codes have been called.

What Key Stakeholders Most Appreciated about the Model

The competency process increased staff accountability. Staff members could seek out the method of validation that was most appealing to them, making the education a more meaningful experience. The employees who did not participate in the engaging activities did not have good feedback about the competency. Hopefully they will plan better and take advantage of earlier opportunities for validating their competency in years to come.

> *Since implementation of the competency, restraint episodes have decreased by almost 50%, and no inappropriate codes have been called.*

Overcoming Our Most Difficult Competency Hurdles

The biggest difficulty we had was distinguishing between true competency issues and lack of compliance.

Initial involvement was a challenge. The longer the new process is in place, the more staff are getting involved in the planning stages. It took some time for staff members to recognize that they have the ability to bring to light current issues on the unit that need to be addressed through the competency process.

Benefits to Individuals and the Organization

Staff seem more engaged and empowered. They have realized that their leaders will listen to their concerns and help them develop ways to improve through education.

Staff members now have more concern for wanting to do things the right way. The employees who took advantage of the earlier opportunities for validation, which included a more fun and interactive approach, have been willing to discuss issues openly and seem to have more job satisfaction. The number of engaged

REFLECTIONS FROM ORGANIZATIONS THAT HAVE USED THE WRIGHT COMPETENCY MODEL

employees outweighs the number of employees who do the bare minimum, a huge shift from prior to implementing the new competency method.

Annette Dailey, MSN, RN
KHN Learning System Manager

Michele Kolp, MSN, RN
Nursing Professional Development Specialist
Kettering Behavioral Medical Center

The Goal Was Saving Resources; the Outcome Was a Valuable Competency Process

UnityPoint Health Des Moines
Des Moines, Iowa

This regional health care system which provides care to nine geographic locations in the Midwest saved financial and time resources and made their competency assessment process relevant to professional practice by decentralizing validation and aligning competencies with organizational initiatives and quality concerns.

Motivation for Changing Our Competency Assessment Process

The competency program at UnityPoint Health (formerly Iowa Health Des Moines) had never been standardized; each specialty used a different process to select and verify competencies. This was inefficient from both a people and financial resource standpoint.

Where We Were and Where We Wanted to Go

Historically, staff spent hours on "skills day" being educated on and verifying the same skills or concepts annually because we "have always done it that way." A goal was to save financial resources by reducing hours spent on skills day and verifying competencies via evidence of daily work and in the departments.

From a regulatory standpoint, our employee records confirming verification of competencies were inconsistent. Our various educators did not record competencies in the same way. We also did not associate competencies with specific organizational initiatives or quality concerns.

Our goal was to ensure that our competencies were aligned with what benefited the organization as well as the individual clinician. We spent 2013 as a pilot year, implementing the Wright Competency Assessment process with our inpatient nursing staffs.

What Key Stakeholders Most Appreciated about the Model

Holding staff accountable for their own performance and competencies was a new concept to many staff and leaders in our organization. Some departments did this very well; other departments were inconsistent. We engaged Human Resources early on in this journey to develop a shared understanding of how the new model would impact our annual evaluation process, part of which is based on meeting expectations for competency. We surveyed three groups following our pilot year: staff, educators, and managers. We had about a 33% response rate; approximately 75% of respondents thought that the Wright Competency Assessment Model was a good approach. The two most common favorable comments supported the reduction of skills day hours and the increased staff accountability.

> *The two most common favorable comments supported the reduction of skills day hours and the increased staff accountability.*

Overcoming Our Most Difficult Competency Hurdles

We are rolling our new model out to all nursing staff, inpatient and outpatient. We hope to improve our categorization and archiving process so that educators can share their work. Our unit-based educators are struggling to align the most valuable verification technique with the identified competency. We hope to involve the Clinical Education Specialists sooner in reviewing the competencies selected and the verification techniques the unit-based educators are planning to utilize. Lastly, we realized that the cycle period we used for the selection of competencies and corresponding verification methods is too short. The steering team needs more time to finalize the competencies before they "go to print." This time may shrink as the organization as a whole becomes better at understanding the various verification techniques and how to use them effectively.

It was a struggle for most departments to identify their most critical competencies. We still have several units with 10 competencies, which include the four global competencies for all of nursing. Since a specific global competency for all of nursing may get added throughout the year, deadlines for completion can get confusing. We are really trying to emphasize that the department competencies for each year need to be specific to a department quality or performance need, and that departments do not need to have 13 or 14 competencies, as was the standard in the past.

> We are really trying to emphasize that the department competencies for each year need to be specific to a department quality or performance need.

Benefits to Individuals and the Organization

The accountability piece of Donna Wright's model is being applied in our organization, even beyond competency assessment. We are seeing staff being held more accountable when rolling out new initiatives, in follow-up to regulatory corrective actions, and in the competency-based orientation process for new hires. Some of our staff did not meet expectations for competency assessment during this pilot year and consequently did not get a merit increase or bonus. We're confident that these consequences for not meeting expectations will prevent this from happening again, with them or other staff.

Educators are collaborating at a higher level as they share verification techniques and work on other educational projects.

Cherry R. Shogren, MSN, RN, NE-BC,
Director, Clinical Professional Development
UnityPoint Health Des Moines

A Very Diverse System Plus Regulatory Requirements for Education Required a Streamlined System

Norton Healthcare
Louisville, Kentucky

This system of hospitals, intermediate care centers and an outpatient center received several certifications that added required education to an already cumbersome list of competencies. They adopted the Wright Competency Assessment Model, placing accountability with each professional nurse, in collaboration with nurse managers.

Motivation for Changing Our Competency Assessment Process

Norton Healthcare (NHC) in Louisville, Kentucky is one of the area's leading health care providers. It consists of five hospitals (including Kosair Children's Hospital), a pediatric outpatient medical center, 12 intermediate care centers, and more than 90 physician practice locations.

Prior to the implementation of the Wright Competency Assessment Model, the nursing competencies were categorized into: core competencies (those that needed to be validated by every nurse in the inpatient, outpatient surgical, and oncology services); specialty-specific competencies; and facility-specific competencies. Altogether, these competencies filled five 8×14 pages. Skills were tested year after year whether they were a problem or not. The focus was on validating technical skills and doing web-based tests. There were inconsistencies between facilities in how validation was performed and in how staff members were held accountable.

Where We Were and Where We Wanted to Go

The competency process had become burdensome, to say the least. It was big on quantity, but not always in quality. NHC was in the process of receiving certification from The Joint Commission for several specialty services (including stroke, breast, and orthopedic). With each certification came education requirements that were actualized as competencies, adding to the list.

> *In her humorous way, Donna showed us what was needed to improve our process. (She had us at, "checky, checky, checky!")*

The competency process was usually led by the unit educators. We needed a seamless process with managers working with their staff to own the process. There had to be a better way to identify competencies and to differentiate competencies from regulatory requirements. Employees needed to be accountable for their own competency process. Documentation of competency validation needed to be computerized.

Then, Donna Wright came and the light was turned on! Donna was asked to be the main speaker for Norton Healthcare's Nurses Week Presentation, in May, 2012. In her humorous way, Donna showed us what was needed to improve our process. (She had us at, "checky, checky, checky!")

In July, 2012, a committee began the work of adopting the Wright Competency Assessment Model. Meeting every two weeks, the committee adapted the model and incorporated Swanson's Theory of Caring (Swanson, 1991) and Benner's Novice to Expert Theory (Benner, 2001). We developed a competency assessment form and verification methods. Competencies were divided into those that needed performance validation, those that had to be learned because of a new process or equipment, and those that were required by regulatory standards. We constructed examples for the RN, PCA, unit secretary, and surgical tech roles. Once the conceptual work was completed, we presented the NHC Competency Model to the System Nursing Executive Team of chief nursing officers, which they accepted. We then presented our model to four different focus groups and modified it to incorporate their suggested changes. The final NHC Competency Model debuted at our 2013 Nurses Week celebration, then for each of the facilities' nursing leadership groups and the Practice Governance Council.

Since the nurse managers' role in the competency process was changing, Donna Wright was invited back to speak with the nursing leadership of NHC (nurse managers, directors, educators, and CNOs). The focus of the discussion was their leadership and accountability in the process. After Donna's presentation in

REFLECTIONS FROM ORGANIZATIONS THAT HAVE USED THE WRIGHT COMPETENCY MODEL

September, all nursing staff attended a required in-service on the new competency model. Finally, in November, 2013, the nurse managers began meeting with their staffs to identify the competencies pertinent to their unit, based on performance improvement data. The competency period for 2014 was identified as March 1 through October 31, 2014.

What Key Stakeholders Most Appreciated about the Model

From the focus groups to the leadership in-services to the staff in-services, the value for all with this model is the accountability of the employee for his or her own competency, and the direction and follow-through by the nurse manager. In addition, the employees liked the participation in and accountability for identification of the competencies by unit-based teams.

Overcoming Our Most Difficult Competency Hurdles

The major hurdle encountered was the shift in direction for the competency process from the educators to the nurse managers. Some educators wanted to continue to control the process, and some nurse managers wanted their educators to continue to control the process. Educators were encouraged to be part of the identification of competencies within the unit-based teams and to be resources throughout the process. Additional problems revolved around communication issues, making sure that all staff heard consistent information.

Benefits to Individuals and the Organization

Benefits already observed include a better understanding by both staff and management that there are more ways to validate competencies than check-offs and tests; staff members appreciate having a choice of what verification method best fits who they are and what they do. The accountability and the focus on critical thinking and interpersonal skills built into the model contribute to the professional growth of the nurse. Adapting the Wright Competency Assessment Model

At its best, staff and management will be more engaged, accountable, timely, and will grow professionally.

has been exciting, rewarding, and exhausting. At the very basic level, it is a significant improvement over our previous cumbersome process. At its best, staff and management will be more engaged, accountable, timely, and will grow professionally. Finally, patients will have the benefit of continuing to receive quality care from competent caregivers.

Sharon Conway, MSN, RN, NE-BC
Director, Patient Care Operations
Norton Healthcare

From Education as the Solution to Every Performance Problem, to Demonstrating the Skills Needed to Do the Job

North Kansas City Hospital
North Kansas City, Missouri

This metropolitan medical center built a competency assessment model focused on outcomes, and expanded beyond technical skills, knowing that the majority of patient outcomes are determined by nurses' interpersonal and critical thinking skills. Staff involvement in the total process minimized resistance to change.

Motivation for Changing Our Competency Assessment Process

We were tired of competency assessment being inefficient, ineffective, redundant, and a waste of time for everyone involved. We realized that there were situations and policies involving regulatory standards that restricted our competency assessment process. We wanted to create a competency assessment system that focused on outcomes rather than on the process.

Our current validation process was stagnant, with staff often just parroting information, not demonstrating competency. We had been conducting skills fairs the same way for years, fulfilling the need for assessing technical skills but costing the hospital nearly $500,000 annually. At one time the skills fair was effective, but not anymore. The number of what we called competencies was unmanageable, and they were not a valid assessment of nurses' knowledge, skills, abilities, and behaviors needed to carry out their jobs. We wanted to make competency assessment more meaningful to the nurses and to make them individually accountable for demonstrating competency.

Where We Were and Where We Wanted to Go

Historically, all staff needed to prove competency by reading an educational PowerPoint or policy and then completing an online forced-answer test. Most of these competencies were created as a result of an error or poor outcome that was actually related to compliance of one individual or one unit; others were created due to a new initiative being implemented within the organization. We also held a skills fair twice a year that addressed national patient safety goals and high-risk/low-volume nursing skills, most of which were repeated at each skills fair with minor updating. Before each skills fair we provided study guides that spoon-fed the information and skills being tested, as if staff would wake up one morning and forget how to perform an everyday skill they'd been performing for years.

> *The majority of patient outcomes are determined by nurses' interpersonal and critical thinking skills.*

Our dream was a competency assessment system designed and managed by the nurses who deliver direct patient care, and their leaders. We desired a fluid process that focused on outcomes and the delivery of efficient and effective care, and supported our organization's mission, vision, and values. We also aspired to create an environment that supported positive employee behavior and placed accountability for competence in the hands of the employee.

Another of our goals was to focus on skills other than technical and clinical skills. The majority of patient outcomes are determined by nurses' interpersonal and critical thinking skills: communicating about a patient's condition, providing customer service, listening to and advocating for patients and their families, managing conflict, solving problems, and managing time, to name just a few. We believe that mastery of these relational skills is what really improves patient outcomes.

What Key Stakeholders Most Appreciated about the Model

Staff like being able to drive their own competency bus. Each unit met at least once to determine the changes, needs, and outcomes for their patient population and, viola!—competencies pertinent to the care "my unit" provides were born. When competency assessment relates directly to what staff does every day, it is more meaningful to everyone involved. Many nurse leaders were pleased about the new streamlined process, clearly defined expectations, and focus on critical thinking and interpersonal skills.

Within one month of implementation a staff nurse stated, "I really like this process. I have to really think about this information prior to doing the crossword puzzle. I learned more about strokes by doing the crossword puzzle than I ever have before."

Clinical nurse educators were thrilled that the focus of competency assessment shifted from education as the solution to every performance issue to actual competency verification! The focus is now on the skills required to perform a job, and education is provided only for those who do not meet the competency requirement.

Overcoming Our Most Difficult Competency Hurdles

Implementing change has a reputation for being difficult. We have found that people are not resistant to change; rather, they are resistant to being controlled. From the very beginning, we worked rigorously to involve the nurses affected by the change. We used a special group of nurses (clinical liaisons) and immediately addressed the concerns and questions of all of the nurses who would be involved in the change. Explaining the benefits of this new way of identifying competency was an exhausting process in an organization with 1,300 nurses and a small Nursing Education Department. We attended staff meetings and leadership meetings, conducted road shows on the units, made a video introducing our new process, and invited Donna Wright to present a workshop and energize our organization's nurse leaders.

> *We have found that people are not resistant to change; rather, they are resistant to being controlled.*

Some units had a difficult time understanding that competency identification needed to be individualized for their unit. Another hurdle was that many nurses had trouble letting go of certain competencies they had done for years. Some nurses wanted to recommend competencies for other units.

It was also a challenge to articulate the new competency assessment process to nurse managers and nurse leaders who did not attend the educational offering presented by Donna and who, therefore, did not possess an informed vision of the change being implemented. For this endeavor to be successful, it was necessary that everyone involved, from nursing leadership to the newly hired graduate nurse, understand the definition of competency and the process of competency assessment.

COMPETENCY ASSESSMENT FIELD GUIDE

Benefits to Individuals and the Organization

The greatest benefit is that nurses in our organization have a voice in identifying what is important in their role. Nurses are no longer asked to verify competency of a skill that they already perform successfully or that does not pertain to their role or unit. Nurses have options to verify competency, including discussion groups, which are totally new concepts in our organization, and they love that they have choices! Staff attending early discussion groups indicated they benefitted greatly from sharing ideas with their peers and, given the mix of day and night shift attendees, light was shed on the uniqueness of each shift and how they could best help one another. This was especially evident during the pain management competency discussion group involving the timing of medications for the patient in the morning (prior to therapy) and what the night nurse could do to help the day nurse address the patient's pain. Overall, nurses' feedback has been extremely positive, and we have heard comments such as, "It makes me think," and, "This really helped, much more than the skills fair did." Our new competency assessment process is much more meaningful to everyone within the Nursing Division at North Kansas City Hospital.

> *Nurses are no longer asked to verify competency of a skill that they already perform successfully or that does not pertain to their role or unit.*

Michelle Lane, MSN, RN, CMSRN, NE-BC
Nursing Education Manager
North Kansas City Hospital

Discovering the True Meaning of Competency Makes for Authentic, Rewarding Assessment

St. Luke's Health System
Boise, Idaho

This system of seven medical centers, a tumor center, and a children's hospital drilled down to the meaningful parts of each of their competencies and what would demonstrate that competency. Involvement and investment from the staff gave the ability to identify what the assessment needs really are for each competency.

Motivation for Changing Our Competency Assessment Process

Frustration: overwhelming mandatory requirements that became the educator's problem to solve.

The definition of insanity: doing something the same way as before and expecting different outcomes. The logic of focusing attention on something you have identified in your job as a problem, not spending time and energy on something that is not. These were the issues that brought us to change our competency assessment process. The Wright Competency Assessment Model utilizes adult learning principles; its goals are attainable and valuable. It holds people accountable . . . the right people.

Where We Were and Where We Wanted to Go

Our existing system consisted of numerous on-line modules with tests, and skills labs where staff members could arrive unprepared and be walked through the process and checked off. It was the educator's responsibility to ensure that everyone was competent (meaning they attended skills labs or were checked off).

We wanted a competency assessment process that reflects a rapidly changing work environment, and that develops critical thinking, problem solving, and analysis. We wanted it to focus on meaningful and pertinent needs: engaged, adult learning. And we wanted nurses to be accountable and responsible for their professional practice and education, from the inside out (empowerment and ownership).

Our system needed a built-in evaluation/improvement process. In theory, if the metrics determine that a function or skill should be a mandatory competency, next year's metrics should show improvement in that function or skill, if the competency education was successful. If metrics for that function or skill still show a problem, the education needs to be re-evaluated.

What Key Stakeholders Most Appreciated about the Model

At one of the clinics, an RN who heard about the new competency model rolled her eyes and said, "One more flavor of the month." Her leader asked her to read Donna Wright's book and come back with some recommendations on how this might work. When she returned, she was quite passionate about the process. She said, "You know, this is really smart... I think we should try this; it will make a difference."

Once we understood it, and saw that it was working, what more could we ask for? This system works and reveals things that could and should be improved. As an educator, I am all for putting power back in the hands of those "in the trenches." I think giving people choices will empower and excite them.

Giving people choices will empower and excite them.

We implemented the Donna Wright system for the transfusion service in the lab. Based on voting by the technologists, we chose to measure competency in working up a warm autoantibody. We used evidence of daily work, exemplars, and two case studies presented in stages (information, followed by the question, "What would you do next?"). The competency exercise/evaluation was a success. The Medical Lab Scientist staff found it quite educational, and I heard some of them say that working through the competency helped remove some fear of the procedure.

There is a great deal of creative thinking required at the outset, because evaluating performance of a multi-step, if-this-then-that, critical thinking task needs to be meaningful; designing the competencies was not easy. This is the step that seems to make or break the system. This is the step that requires experts at the task. We set up a flow chart for the process and identified pieces that were absolutely necessary. This was our guide in measuring success.

Attending Donna's competency webinar taught me the importance of presentations, and how they should be implemented to assess competency. Donna stated that you should know the information three times better than your audience. That surely sent home a message that I need to know my stuff before I present.

Overcoming Our Most Difficult Competency Hurdles

Things had been the same at St. Luke's for so long that imagining it differently was a challenge. I never knew that skills labs were *not* the only way to go until learning about Donna Wright's model. Looking at competency without the structure we were raised with was a huge paradigm shift. We struggled; we had to keep going back to making it meaningful and useful—otherwise why were we requiring it?

For some, the new model was not prescriptive enough, but others saw that as a benefit. It relied on a systematic process that included prioritization of competencies, which was easy to understand. Drilling down to the meaningful part of what each competency is and what would demonstrate that competency was sometimes difficult, but that is where we found the gold. People were engaged, and have started getting very creative with validations. However, it takes energy, time, and trust. In this process, we learned a lot. Some units didn't trust the process; they just wanted to be told what to do.

It took some trial and error before it became clear that, first of all, the target workgroup absolutely had to be defined. For the autoantibody procedure, since some labs rarely perform transfusions, designing a one-size-fits-all competency evaluation simply will not work. We also learned that educators may not always be the best choice to work out the competency strategy. It was hard for many to separate competency and education.

The roles of implementers, supervisors, managers, and educators were not defined specifically enough at the outset.

Benefits to Individuals and the Organization

Involvement and investment from the staff gave us the ability to identify what the assessment needs really are for each competency: just-in-time education, review, or mandatory competency. The model saves time, and it really is the best way of knowing someone is competent to do his or her job. It allows the unique needs of a job in a certain area to be addressed—no longer the shotgun approach. We all have a better understanding of what the problems really are. Through dialog we determined that what we thought was the issue was sometimes just a symptom. It helped us focus on the real problem.

One unanticipated benefit was that by putting responsibility on the participants and forcing them to go to the standards of practice, we revealed some weaknesses in those standards!

We are using more simulations, an improvement over employees only attending a skills lab—they have to be prepared and involved. Air St. Luke's requires all flight personnel and ground paramedics to give a presentation once a year about a specific patient or flight, including a component of evidence-based practice with research articles. Donna Wright's perspective on how physicians use this tool in educating one another is a great example of why we as nurses should do the same.

Paula Lewis, RN-C, BSN, MBA
Program Manager Clinical Learning
St. Luke's Health System

Within this same system, St. Luke's Children's Hospital in Boise, Idaho, took the Wright Competency Model by the horns and realized their own huge success. Their inspiring story is next!

A Story of Cost Savings . . . and Tenacity!

St. Luke's Children's Hospital
Boise, Idaho

This children's hospital, part of St. Luke's Health System, moved from volumes of modules to a stronger, more cost-effective competency process.

Motivation for Changing Our Competency Assessment Process

We wanted to save money, time, and energy.

Where We Were and Where We Wanted to Go

Our competency program used to consist of a 1-pound packet of modules and a 12-hour day of skills lab. The PICU was divided into two groups: the "spring" group and the "fall" group. So this cumbersome pack of paper and set of extra 12-hour shifts occurred once a year for the participants, and twice a year for the instructors. The process was costly and extremely time-consuming. The modules were the same every year, so many staff kept a completed copy in their mailboxes to simply transfer answers from. I felt that the process was ineffective at best

My vision for the unit was a cleaner process; one that was clear, concise, and relevant. Then along came Donna Wright and her *Ultimate Guide to Competency Assessment*. It all seemed so simple and made so much sense. I was captivated by the thought of changing competencies every year and of a system that stressed the importance of limiting the number of competencies. Our current system kept adding new modules but never dropped archaic ones. The time commitment kept getting longer and longer.

What Key Stakeholders Most Appreciated about the Model

The Wright Competency Assessment Model focuses on the new, the problematic, and the life-threatening. It stresses keeping the total number of competencies to fewer than ten and giving multiple methods to validate each one. Again, so logical: employees can choose the options for completion that work best for them, which makes learning more meaningful.

In this day and age of medical and financial difficulties, I think that the biggest advantage to adopting the Wright Competency Model was simply dollars. Cost savings were realized from reductions in time, scheduling, paper, and staff resources.

The feedback was positive. The staff engagement was encouraging. The learning was more solid. Communication in the unit was sparked. Staff members were actually engaged in the learning.

Overcoming Our Most Difficult Competency Hurdles

Those who claimed that it couldn't be done and people with the "This is the way we've always done it" mentality argued against the change. Still, we pushed on with the thought of trying it for a year, just to see.

Of course we didn't do everything right the first time around, but we took what we learned from our first year and applied it to the second year.

Benefits to Individuals and the Organization

Our goal is to have a system that makes sense and that gives the staff useful, take-away knowledge. We will continue to "work the process." It just makes sense.

Michele Schwister, PICU RN, BSN, CCRN
Bedside Nurse, Relief Charge, Chair of the Education Committee
St. Luke's Children's Hospital

A Paradigm Shift (and a Creative Automotive Theme) Brought Accountability and Engagement

Children's Mercy Hospital
Kansas City, Missouri

This urban pediatric medical center used the Wright Competency Assessment Model to change their paradigm of competency education and assessment from a leader-driven system to staff-driven accountability.

Motivation for Changing Our Competency Assessment Process

Several nurses from our organization, including unit-based educators, education specialists, and a practice manager, attended a conference, "Slaying the Competency Monster: Making Competency Assessment Fun and Easy!" presented by Donna Wright. During the conference it became apparent to us that there was a better way to conduct our competency program.

Where We Were and Where We Wanted to Go

Our history had always been to repeat the same competencies year after year in house-wide skills days. Over the years, the competency lists grew longer and longer; no skills were deleted, only added. Departments outside the nursing division (e.g., infection control and safety) expected to have their identified education needs and projects added to the list. The result was lists that could contain 30 or more competencies. The same skills were repeated each year. While it was a popular method, allowing staff to complete their competency list in one session, it was labor-intensive, costly, and out of control.

COMPETENCY ASSESSMENT FIELD GUIDE

After hearing about Donna's competency assessment model, we dreamed of a meaningful and more empowering competency process. There was organizational support to evaluate and improve our process. An interprofessional steering committee that included directors, educators, and advanced practice professionals started by reading Donna's book and envisioning how to implement the model at Children's Mercy. Believing that competencies are ever-changing, we developed the Competency Assessment Roadtrip (CAR) to model our competency journey. See **Figure B.1** below.

Step	Action
1.	Gather your QI data and schedule a meeting with your competency workgroup (director, educator, representatives from the job classification). Optional: You may include your "Trip Advisor."
2.	Complete the *Worksheet for Identifying Ongoing Competencies* with the competency workgroup. This will include all positions reporting to the Director/Manager: Unit Secretaries, Techs, etc. *** When considering staff with multiple roles: Focus on "what makes sense for them to do." If this can't be decided at the director/manager level, then consult the CAR Steering Committee for recommendation. Remember: no more than 10 competencies per job position - POC testing will be one of the competencies.
3.	Once the top competencies are identified, begin developing the verification methods. Goal is to have more than one verification method for each competency. Examples of the verification methods are found on Scope > PCS >Competency Assesment Roadtrip > Resources
4.	After the competencies have been identified, complete the annual employee form and distribute to all staff in that job position. Make sure that all staff have the materials they need to complete the verification methods (access to tests, case studies, etc).

Step	Action
5.	Overall completion date for this year's competencies is November 30th. Staff will complete the annual employee form and submit their supporting evidence for each identified job position competency to the unit/department supervisor as instructed. Note: Please refer to the Competency Validation Policy regarding staff who do not comply with the November 30th deadline for their annual competencies.
6.	Each calendar year, employees are expected to complete annual competencies on their annual employee form. As new employees start throughout the calendar year, they are expected to complete the orientation competency validation tool (OCVT). The following calendar year, they will complete the annual competencies.

7.	Competency Considerations can include:
	
	Back to Basics Initiatives Communication with Families
	Medication scheduling Safety Issues (Incident Reports)
	Central Line Blood Stream Infections (CLBSI) Downtime Processes
	    Service Excellence
	NDNQI data Emergency Preparedness
	Clinical Documentation Audits Skin Care/Pressure Ulcers
	NRC Picker results Falls
	Collaborative Projects (with outside organizations) Unit Quality Projects
	    Hospital Acquired Conditions
	Restraints

8.	Documentation: Units directors will maintain a copy of the *Worksheet for Identifying Ongoing Competencies*, the annual employee form for each position, and documents created for competency verification methods.
9.	Send copies of the *Worksheet for Identifying Ongoing Competencies*, the annual employee form for each position, and documents created for competency verification methods to your CAR Trip Advisor.

COMPETENCY ASSESSMENT FIELD GUIDE

Step	Action
10.	The CAR Steering Committee is here to help! Please feel free to email the Competency Transformation Steering Committee distribution group.

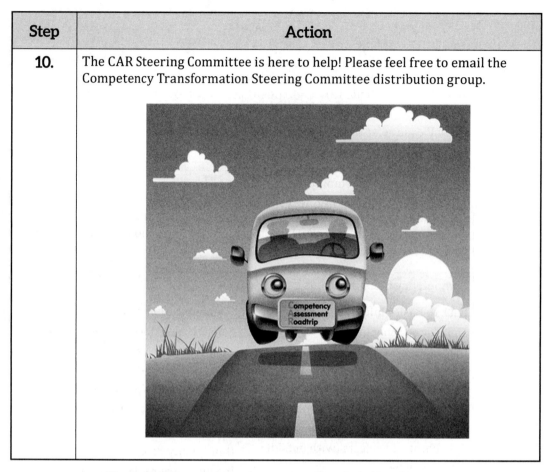

Figure B.1: Competency Assessment Roadtrip (CAR) Model

What Key Stakeholders Most Appreciated about the Model

Staff initially appreciated not having to come in on a day off to check off their competencies, as well as the more manageable and meaningful list of competencies. Staff members were engaged in the process of identifying their unit's specific competencies. Staff also appreciated that Donna was brought in to share and further explain her model.

The Steering Committee developed a presentation using parallels to automobile themes. The presentation stressed that competency is a journey that needs preparation. Staff members will be supported by a Pit Crew (educators, managers, and the employees themselves). Ongoing competencies will be organized like scheduled maintenance for a car. A service center is staffed by the CAR Steering Committee to help review competency tools and provide other needed help, and Trip Advisor (aka Roadside Assistance) is available to assist in planning annual competencies.

Overcoming Our Most Difficult Competency Hurdles

The new model was a paradigm shift that required leaders, staff, and educators to change the way they viewed accountability and competencies. Our history had been leader-driven competencies. Our CAR model has shifted the paradigm to staff-driven competencies and accountability. This has not been without some angst. Some leaders are fearful of giving up control, and some staff members are afraid of accepting accountability for their practice. The model is moving us toward a stronger shared governance/collaborative approach to identification and demonstration of competency.

> *The model is moving us toward a stronger shared governance/collaborative approach to identification and demonstration of competency.*

Benefits to Individuals and the Organization

The benefit to CAR hasn't yet been fully recognized; however the overall paradigm shift is a move in the right direction. Some departments have fully embraced the model, noting their appreciation that staff can select and complete their verification methods at their own pace. Staff also report being engaged in the unit-based committees that determine the annual competencies.

Ellen Kisling, MSN, RN
Director of Education

Michele Fix, MSN, RN, NE-BC
Manager of Clinical Informatics & Practice
Children's Mercy Hospital

"We Now Talk in Competency Language"

Virginia Commonwealth University Health System
Richmond, Virginia

In this teaching hospital, part of a large university medical system, inconsistencies in competency assessment between units, disciplines, and full- and part-time employees were addressed in a new system that has changed the culture of accountability for validating competencies and the language used to address performance issues.

Motivation for Changing Our Competency Assessment Process

Way back in 2003, our Joint Commission HR team recommended development of an organizational plan for competency assessment. Based on this recommendation, Donna Wright was invited to speak at Grand Rounds and consult on the topic of competency assessment. During that visit, Donna met with clinical nursing staff, nurse leadership, and Human Resources leadership teams. Following this visit, competency assessment was redefined organization-wide. Donna was asked to return to consult with HR and nurse leaders to begin the process of making major revisions to the existing approach to competency assessment to begin to establish a consistent framework. Prior to Donna's visit, many department leaders and staff members misunderstood what competency assessment entailed. Departments utilized a checklist approach in an attempt to document ability to perform what was identified as desired skill at a single point in time. Method of validation was a simple return demonstration in a classroom-like setting.

A formal organization-wide competency assessment plan was initiated in 2004, with final completion in 2006. Identification and prioritization of ongoing competencies resulted from an assessment of new, changed, high-risk, and problematic performance elements. Departments embraced a multidimensional approach to validating critical thinking, technical, and interpersonal aspects of performance as part of ongoing professional practice. The reason for competence assessment was documented and the method of validation expanded to include in-service, return demonstration, exemplar, presentation, test, observation of performance, case study, and alternate methods as appropriate.

Where We Were and Where We Wanted to Go

The process of assessing competency was overwhelming to leaders who were involved in ensuring and documenting staff competence for regulatory agencies such as The Joint Commission (TJC). Skills fairs were time-consuming and left unit educators wondering if their employees were really competent. According to HR, nursing was the only area focused on competency assessment. When department leaders talked about competency, they understood evaluation, but not the competency assessment process. To address this knowledge gap, The Joint Commission HR group focused on physician competencies, then nursing, followed by other clinical disciplines, then non-clinical areas such as central sterile supply. Competency assessment is now common language throughout the organization.

Various units performed competencies differently, which was challenging for nurses who transferred between them.

An overarching goal was to make the process easier to understand and consistent across the organization. Various units performed competencies differently, which was challenging for nurses who transferred between them. One of our initial goals was to establish broad foundational competencies and then specialty competencies.

The timing of competency assessment was another aspect to consider, since employee anniversary dates would be different from dates of completing competencies. Establishing a standard point in time to document competency and a standard cycle for validating competencies was important. We incorporated competency validation into annual performance appraisals in 2007. The HR Joint Commission subgroup walked each department through this new process. During the months of December through March, departments developed competencies for their areas and submitted them to the HR subgroup for approval and checking for errors in language, validation techniques, etc. During April through November, units completed their competencies using a variety of methods of validation. The HR subgroup determined what actions would be taken for individuals who did not complete the competency assessment. Competency information was maintained on a spreadsheet by HR to keep leaders abreast of competency status for each staff member. This strategy helped identify actual and potential issues with the newly implemented process.

Competency assessment for part-time employees had previously been inconsistent because these employees were often not present when the skills fairs were being held. But now, exemplars were an option for demonstrating competence, and staff were accustomed to writing exemplars of practice through the organization's clinical ladder program.

Units have moved away from competency fairs. The responsibility to complete identified competencies is shifted from the manager to the employees, who are expected to complete their competencies during April through November using a variety of predetermined methods of validation. Gaps can now be identified through competency needs assessments.

The competency assessment cycle has shifted from the employee's anniversary date to the standard cycle of competency assessment. During this transition period, if the employee was making progress towards completing competencies and had completed them the previous year, it would be recorded that he or she had "passed" competency on the annual performance appraisal.

What Key Stakeholders Most Appreciated about the Model

Having everyone on the same page, using the same definitions for competency assessment and the same template/structure, has made the process much more manageable. A standard framework for competency validation allows for unit/department individualization of content. The tools are adaptable to manual or electronic systems of documentation and recording.

Overcoming Our Most Difficult Competency Hurdles

People struggle with learning on the fly and marrying day-to-day practice with competency. We need to identify problem-prone areas and work with them. We need to better utilize performance improvement data as the driving force for our competencies. It is important to conduct focus groups to see what challenges different groups are facing. We need to enhance our orientation to the competency assessment process for staff and leaders (especially interim managers/leaders). And, we need succession training and mentoring to keep the system running seamlessly.

Benefits to Individuals and the Organization

The change itself has helped people get over their initial fears that the new process could not be as easy as it sounded or would at least be as difficult as it had been in the past, as well as whether TJC would really accept it. After several successful TJC surveys, this is no longer a concern.

> *It's second nature now, when addressing a performance issue to determine if this is a competency issue or a commitment issue.*

We now talk in competency language. It's second nature now, when addressing a performance issue to determine if this is a competency issue or a commitment issue (i.e., does the person not know how to do something, is unable to do it correctly for some reason, or is choosing not to do it correctly?). Our performance management decision tree uses these principles in determining if a problem that occurred was related to a deficit in knowledge or process vs. factors the person could control.

Walter Lewanowicz, MN, BSc, RN-BC
Nurse Educator, Department of Education & Professional Development

Ellen Derry, MA, BSN, RN-BC, CPN
Director, Education and Professional Development

Donna Steigleder, BSN, RN
Director of Employee Relations
Virginia Commonwealth University Health System

A Program that Truly Validates Competency also Enhances the Patient Experience, Patient Safety, and Nurse Satisfaction

Morton Plant Mease Health Care (part of BayCare Health System)
Clearwater, Florida

This community health care system's new competency assessment process contains several creative and courageous elements: "No Spoon Feeding," acceptance of error as a way to uncover what needs attention, and clearly stated consequences for non-compliance.

Motivation for Changing Our Competency Assessment Process

Before we implemented the Wright Competency Assessment Model, we had annual skills fairs. During skills fairs, we identified that there seemed to be gaps in proficiency of the nurses. Additionally, our methodology of teaching the nurses could vary. A less than confident nurse might defer to a teammate for assistance. Our desire was to elevate each individual team member's knowledge and their confidence in that knowledge. Skills fairs just were not achieving that for us.

Skills fairs had long proven undesirable for several reasons. The annual skills fairs:

- Only happen once a year
- Are not the best use of staff resources

- Didn't achieve the desired outcome of a standard expectation of knowledge

- Could be intimidating, bringing stress and pressure to what ideally should be a collaborative learning environment

- Did not promote accountability (Educators would teach instead of assess, and provide one-on-one in-services.)

- Did not accommodate different learning styles

- Were not tailored to the particular skills needed or utilized on a regular basis by a particular nurse (e.g., not every nurse puts in PICC lines)

Where We Were and Where We Wanted to Go

We established a goal of a competency assessment that would enable nurses to learn, feel confident in their abilities, be acknowledged for what they already knew, and participate in determining how they validated their own competence. We felt that if we could establish a program that truly validated competency, we would improve the patients' experience, as well as patient safety with improved nurse satisfaction as another important result.

We had visions of a process with a strong foundation in adult learning principles. We would achieve this by building a program that would:

- Standardize performance expectations

- Support employee accountability

- Respect individual employees' learning styles

- Promote a collaborative and individualized learning environment that enabled people to exercise choice in the methodology of learning activity selection

What Key Stakeholders Most Appreciated about the Model

Overall, key stakeholders most appreciated the greater flexibility the model allowed. It gave them access to new ways to demonstrate and validate competency and options for hands-on learning within the competency process itself.

REFLECTIONS FROM ORGANIZATIONS THAT HAVE USED THE WRIGHT COMPETENCY MODEL

New Ways to Demonstrate and Validate Competency

A recent email survey indicated that educators and team members appreciated the ability to personalize the process. The educators really embraced how the new model required them to use new (and invariably more effective) methods of teaching. Teams also appreciated the opportunity to select their preferred way to demonstrate evidence of their competence.

The use of new validation methods was somewhat challenging at first, but was eventually seen as an opportunity for growth and development for everyone involved. Educators initially thought that having team members share their exemplars and case studies or participate in discussion groups, would be met with resistance and cause boredom as nurses waited for their turn to present. They soon realized, however, that the listeners were engaged and eagerly absorbing the information being shared. Exemplars were judged on evidence of the learners' knowledge or understanding needed to demonstrate competence.

> Team members also appreciated the convenience of incorporating validation of their abilities into their daily work. ER was the first unit to do this, with a "Triage Tuesday" and a "Tele Thursday."

Team members also appreciated the convenience of incorporating validation of their abilities into their daily work. ER was the first unit to do this, with a "Triage Tuesday" and a "Tele Thursday." Each nurse submitted a de-identified record of a triage they had completed that day as validation of their competence. Educators and clinical nurse level 2s (CN2s) and clinical nurse level 3s (CN3s) were validated first, and then could validate others. RNs and LPNs enjoyed the recognition of their current performance ability and the fact that there was no test.

An Example of Hands-On Learning in the Competency Assessment Process

Nurses on a Med/Surg Tele unit were the beneficiaries of a creative way to address the skill of responding to a code situation. The educator describes the process this way:

> I noticed that even though our nurses were all CPR-certified, and one or two were ACLS-certified, they were not familiar with setting up the equipment for a code. So as part of the competency, I had the nurses review the policy and procedures. They had time to work with the equipment hands-on. Many of us who are tactile learners have to get in there and do something in order to really

understand it. Then they each did a mock code one-on-one with me, using a manikin and a spare code cart. The mock codes were a bit time-consuming, but valuable. The team said they loved it and were thankful for the opportunity, especially to work one-on-one. I believe that this was a key element because they had to rely on themselves, with no one to coach them. I let them struggle a bit when appropriate and didn't always provide the answer immediately.

As part of this competency assessment, we reviewed:

- Using the bed: CPR release, removing head board, employing back board
- Assembling ambu bag, connecting to flowmeter
- Applying the multifunction stat-padz and set to "monitor"
- Opening the code cart
- Other things: call the physician, ensure patient has working IV site, clear room of extra furniture, move roommate (find someone to stay with roommate if possible) get a portable computer for charting.
- Securing the code cart when code is over

One of my goals is to have all the basics done by the time the Code Team arrives at the bedside. I challenged my team to perfect the process.

This experience made most nurses a great deal more comfortable and proficient with the code blue experience and faster at getting down to the business of saving a life. See **Figure B.2** on the facing page. As part of my action plan, I work with those who indicate residual discomfort on the post-assessment, to strengthen those particular areas.

REFLECTIONS FROM ORGANIZATIONS
THAT HAVE USED THE WRIGHT COMPETENCY MODEL

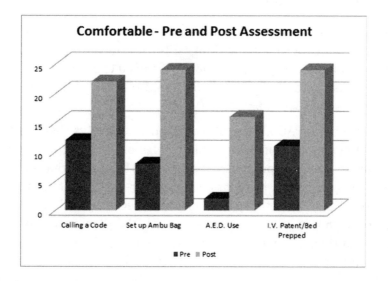

Figure B.2: Nurses' Comfort Pre- and Post-Competency Assessment

Pre-assessment scores show a low level of comfort with required competencies. Post-assessment scores indicate an increase in comfort of greater than 13% for each of the required competencies.

Post-Assessment indicates an increase in comfort with required competencies, greater than 13% in each case.

Overcoming Our Most Difficult Competency Hurdles

The most difficult hurdles we had to overcome were:

- Acceptance of the time-saving benefits of the Wright Competency Model
- Making sure managers were both supported and supportive of the process
- Making sure educators were onboard and supported
- Helping people to see errors as opportunities for learning
- Helping the staff to be 100% accountable for the process

Perception of Time Constraints

Surgery and PACU, two units that don't have a lot of down time, felt that the time required by the new program made things difficult. However, it is also true that if these units are not busy, staff are sent home. We need to study how to address the time issue on these units, but a likely solution discussed was to incorporate the competencies into their workday.

Still, that same OR/PACU team was very quick to involve their leadership and developed one of the most unique competencies on building communication in their team, using the DISC personality profile (2014). They shared their profile results with each other and brought deeper understanding about themselves as communicators. This competency was very well received and is still in use. Initially, some of the nurses feared, incorrectly, that the personality profile was not confidential, and thus declined to participate. When their teammates came back from discussing their results and shared how much they learned, those who did not choose this particular validation were lobbying the educator for the opportunity to get the DISC profile. While it was tempting to provide such a great experience for these "late adopters," the educator stuck to Donna's advice about how to encourage early participation and let them know that that particular validation method was no longer available. Donna's advice is that verification methods slowly become unavailable over time, so that not all options are available by the end of the year. People eventually understand that they will have a better time taking care of their competencies early.

Making Sure Managers are both Supported and Supportive of the Process

Our most challenging hurdle was recognizing that without the manager's leadership, it is difficult to facilitate staff engagement. It is critical that the manager takes the lead in emphasizing the importance of the program and keeps at it with the consistency of a heartbeat.

In our organization, the managers who created the expectation of involvement of their teams in the brainstorming of competencies and involved their leaders in implementing assessment and validation of competence reaped the benefit of team buy-in and good outcomes. One critical care manager quoted a high-performing team member

> *It is critical that the manager takes the lead in emphasizing the importance of the program and keeps at it with the consistency of a heartbeat.*

as saying initially, "I don't care about competence; I just want to do my work." This manager now describes that team member as one of the staunchest supporters of competency assessment.

Best Utilization of Educators

Our educators became the experts and assisted their managers by providing competency topics to bring up at each team meeting. They maintained a constancy of purpose.

New educators have the best chance of success when they have comprehensive support. If the teams found something unappealing about the new plan, some team members attributed the idea of competency assessment to the educators. Some individuals held the educator responsible for identifying the opportunities for improvement. Some team members feared losing their jobs.

The new educators were in the competency champion's office frequently for guidance and support. The new educators are benefiting from heeding the successes of the seasoned educators. They are now experiencing similar success with strong support in the launch and the manager leading the process.

There are two lessons to learn here:

1. The managers need to lead the process.

2. If the manager isn't fully ready to own the process, the new educators on those units need continuous support.

Acceptance of Errors as Learning Opportunities

Another hurdle involved the initial acceptance of error as an opportunity to improve skills. Judgmental environments can lead to one of two adverse outcomes: either nurses will tell you what you want to hear but you will not see improvement, or the nurses will hide errors for fear of losing their jobs. Our organization has quality as a strong element of our culture; we are cognizant that error is usually not attributable to the employee, but rather to the process.

> Our organization has quality as a strong element of our culture; we are cognizant that error is usually not attributable to the employee, but rather to the process.

For example, a very conscientious staff member was responsible for precepting all the non-licensed staff. Her unit elected to focus on intake and output measurement as one of their competencies for their non-licensed staff. The preceptor checked out the demonstration methodology and realized that she had been measuring intake and output incorrectly and had shared the incorrect method during the orientation process. With the organization's support, the team was re-educated. She was devastated, but was supported in rectifying the situation.

Staff Accountability

Our educators emphasized team members' accountability for themselves. We began awarding a crystal spoon to any educator who could share a "No Spoon Feeding" story. At team meetings, educators shared stories of opportunities for improvement. "Spoon feeding" for educators might include such things as extending deadlines, making extra copies, etc. This award kept us cognizant of how this could create more variation from the intended process and increase the requests for such consideration in the future, making the process cumbersome. Others outside of our department began to work to earn a crystal spoon. At least two managers and a respiratory therapist were also recipients of the award. Our goal was to focus on supporting and empowering staff, not enabling them.

> *Our goal was to focus on supporting and empowering staff, not enabling them.*

Benefits to Individuals and the Organization

In our second full year of competency assessment, we have realized three major areas we now emphasize:

- The importance of pre-measurement
- Instilling staff accountability from the start
- Being firm in the tenet of letting the team select what they need to study

It is clear that we should have put pre-measurement at the forefront. You will have outcomes without pre-measurement, but the magnitude of the change that occurs from highlighting a particular competency is not clear without a pre-measurement. Additionally, graphs and numbers help to illustrate the program's success to leadership. A great competency with an excellent plan for validating it, without a pre-measure, is not quantifiable. We now include a pre-measurement element on our face sheet (a form provided to each nurse for recording competence).

REFLECTIONS FROM ORGANIZATIONS
THAT HAVE USED THE WRIGHT COMPETENCY MODEL

The second significant revelation was how the managers ultimately drove us to greater staff accountability. They met with human resources and determined consequences for non-compliance with the new program. It was so important that we included information about consequences on the face sheets, bolded and highlighted. No one will be able to say, "I had no idea participation was important."

Each unit selects its competencies. You can guide them somewhat using data about their current performance on a particular topic, but the unit team ultimately has to own the selection. As we approach our next competency year, we are being lobbied by Six Sigma and specialty departments to make their competencies mandatory. Everything is important, but the teams know what they need to focus on to improve performance in their unique environments.

> *You will have outcomes without pre-measurement, but the magnitude of the change that occurs from highlighting a particular competency is not clear without a pre-measurement.*

Carol Dimura, MSN, RNC
Clinical Education Coordinator for Staff Development
Morton Plant Mease HealthCare, a subsidiary of BayCare Health System

Within the same system, Morton Plant Hospital had a terrific result with the Wright Competency Assessment Model. Their inspiring story follows.

Designing a Skills Fair that Actually Assesses Skills

Morton Plant Hospital
Clearwater, Florida

This community hospital transformed their skills fair and united their team by customizing competency requirements to individual units and fostering individual accountability for completing the assessment process.

Motivation for Changing Our Competency Assessment Process

Organizations have used the skills fair method of competency assessment for many years. It would invariably wind up with a group of nurses around an IV pump, collaboratively programming it correctly. Of course four or five nurses could program the IV pump together correctly. However, this did not demonstrate the competency of the individual nurses. The same seemed true at other skills stations.

We wanted to make the competencies specific to the needs of the individual nursing units. If a particular unit does not accept telemetry patients, there is no point in requiring rhythm recognition assessment as a competency. The Wright Competency Assessment Model suggests that you go through the process of selecting competencies WITH your team—not FOR your team. Doing so helps you identify areas of opportunity that are meaningful to your team, assuring that the competency assessment meets the expectations of their jobs and increases buy-in among team members.

Where We Were and Where We Wanted to Go

Previously, competency assessment was experienced as a rote exercise. We studied for the test, attended the skills fair, and got all our skills checked off. We weren't necessarily proficient in all the skills, but we knew to get help if something came up. We relied on the fact that *someone* on the shift knew how to do the skill.

We wanted a system that was a true demonstration of competency for each individual—a way to validate our proficiency with equipment as well as the rationale behind its use. Competency assessment gave us the "who, what, why, where, and when" of what we were doing as nurses. By engaging nurses in the process, all nurses were given the opportunity to learn and develop. We were committed to being efficient, proficient, and mindful in the design of our competency assessment to include the most recent evidence-based information.

Overcoming Our Most Difficult Competency Hurdles

There was initial resistance to our new ongoing competency model. It looked paper-intensive. It was an expectation that the individual nurse would take responsibility for performance and documentation of competency completion. Once they began to get into the competencies and realized that they didn't have to complete all of the options offered and that they had some choices, the nurses realized that the work was much more manageable, and it was actually fun.

Benefits to Individuals and the Organization

We have demonstrated measurable improvement in our ability to respond to emergency situations. (See **Figure B.2** on page 109.) Our nurses feel much more comfortable and proficient when responding to rapid responses and code blue situations. We also see evidence that what was learned in performing the competencies is retained. Months later nurses continue to reference specific things they learned from these competencies. We no longer just "study for the test." We learn it for life. Now, the whole team responds promptly and without hesitation to any code situation.

Deborah A. Combs RN, BSN
Specialty Educator
Morton Plant Hospital

Decentralized, Time-Sensitive Competency Education

Robert Wood Johnson University Hospital at Somerset
Somerville, New Jersey

This regional medical center changed the focus of competency education from a centralized skills lab validating what had already been validated repeatedly to unit-based validation of competencies that matter: what has changed, and how that change impacts the nurses' practice.

Motivation for Changing Our Competency Assessment Process

The reason we sought to change what we were doing for competency assessment was the sheer magnitude of the skills lab format. The labor-intensive process of developing, updating, setting up, and conducting the skills lab every month outgrew the resources available to implement it. We wanted a more meaningful experience that truly reflected the nurses' practice and decreased the time spent at a central location reviewing the same old processes and taking another quiz on what they already knew. Not every nurse needed to visit every station, and we had to sort out what they did and did not need to do. Additionally, correcting 100 collective quiz questions on the spot for each nurse required a volunteer to correct and an educator to remediate questions answered incorrectly. The list of topics originated from a needs assessment from various stakeholders, but when new policies came along in the course of the year, they were put into the skills lab regardless of whether the bulk of the staff had already attended and would miss the process that had been added. These added-on topics necessitated more quiz questions to see if participants had learned the related skill.

Where We Were and Where We Wanted to Go

For years our format consisted of written competencies at a centralized skills lab that contained poster presentations and policies to back up the information being tested. A reference manual was given to the staff to review before attending the lab, and they were quizzed on the content at each station. In addition, staff performed return demonstrations on IV, PCA, and feeding pumps. There were 20 stations for RNs and six for Patient Care Technicians. Some units such as Maternal Child Health, Critical Care, and the Emergency Department selected some skills that pertained to their scope of practice and conducted unit-specific skills labs.

We decided to abandon the central skills lab format and make the competencies unit-based to reflect what each nursing staff needed to do to demonstrate competency. We questioned managers, educators, and staff about what to include for their respective units. Core competencies such as safety were included for all units in an information packet to be completed online, with unit-specific quizzes generated by the educators for each unit.

This format was a radical departure from the central skills lab, and staff missed the one-to-one interaction with the educators and the "one-stop shopping" to get everything done in one visit. The tracking of completions of the on-line portions plus our composite quizzes did not lend itself to a single completion document. There were still add-on topics at the unit level that we did not know about and consequently were not able to track. We tried to have the skills observation for programming the PCA pump and use of the heparin protocol occur in real time when staff were about to implement the skill; this plan failed because validators were not unit-based and often were not available to go to the unit and observe.

> *This format was a radical departure from the central skills lab, and staff missed the one-to-one interaction with the educators and the "one-stop shopping" to get everything done in one visit.*

After Donna Wright's visit, we were empowered by the nursing executive team to change the competency process. We knew we were still looking at too many topics, and decided to put online only material that reflected changes in policy and practice, as reflected by performance improvement reports, practice problems, or new policies or products. Staff would perform return demonstrations of selected products or processes, and the educators would ask them about the cognitive parts of managing the equipment and assessing the patient. Examples of return demonstrations included peritoneal dialysis, PCA pumps, and a new chest drainage device.

Our hospital's clinical laboratory had a station at the new skills observation to emphasize issues they were having with specimen labeling. The lab person designed a game with questions instead of the usual paper quiz. The work load and stress were decreased, but staff still learned and reviewed important lab processes. This is where we want to be with all our competencies: fewer topics, fewer online quizzes, less redundancy, better tracking, and most importantly, a satisfied staff.

What Key Stakeholders Most Appreciated about the Model

Everyone appreciated the reduction in time spent at a central skills lab, which equated to reduced cost in time and dollars. Staff members bring back a signed competency sheet for management to have available for surveyors and performance evaluations. Staff are less stressed and are actively engaged in the learning. More importantly, the focus is not on what they already know, but on what has changed and how that change impacts their practice. The educators are not telling staff what they should be doing; instead, the focus is on staff telling the educators what they know. We can identify gaps in knowledge and reinforce the correct information in real time.

Overcoming Our Most Difficult Competency Hurdles

The new process was welcomed by staff. The educators still have the problem of deciding what should be assessed as a competency and what should be presented in an in-service, and also are challenged in determining how many topics we want to include. There are still requests to "put it in skills lab."

Our other problem is reaching the 7p.m. to 7a.m. staff with the limited educator resources available at those times. We recognize that we will have to do supplementary skills labs for this group of staff.

Benefits to Individuals and the Organization

The benefits are reduced time, satisfied employees who truly feel the education topics are relevant, managers who can better track the completion of required competencies, and educators who feel in better control of the competency process.

Doris Van Dyke, BSN, RN, B.C.
Nursing Education Specialist
Robert Wood Johnson University Hospital at Somerset

Placing Accountability for Competency Verification with the Professional Nurse Elevates Practice throughout the Organization

Avera McKennan Hospital & University Health Center
Sioux Falls, South Dakota

This health center's new program generated a common language and structure for competency assessment that uses adult learning principles, measures competence rather than providing education, and clearly identifies those who are not engaged.

Motivation for Changing Our Competency Assessment Process

Our previous method of assessing and validating competency was cumbersome and ineffective. Donna Wright came to our organization and gave a presentation on competency assessment and validation that led our nurse leaders to question our practices related to competency assessment and validation, including:

- Roles, responsibility, authority, and accountability of the manager and clinical nurse educator

- The value of hospital-wide competency sessions

- Whether current validation practices impacted outcomes (e.g., Restraint competence validation is conducted yearly, but documentation of restraint use continues to be below standards)

- Whether competency validation was viewed by staff as checking things off on a list or as something that improves practice and outcomes

- Whether the current process rewarded bad behavior and punished good behavior (e.g. scheduling multiple make-up sessions for those who don't complete)

- Whether the current process held staff accountable

Where We Were and Where We Wanted to Go

Many competencies were validated every year through skills fairs. Often the fairs consisted of education rather than validation of competence. Much of the accountability for the process rested with the nurse leaders who were designing the skills fairs, rather than with the staff. A task force assessed the current state, reviewed the literature, read *The Ultimate Guide to Competency Assessment,* and participated in several webinars.

The Wright Model of Competency Assessment encourages unit innovation and creativity, which in itself is educational.

Nurse leaders desired a methodology that truly assessed and validated competence. It became clear that shifting the accountability to the professional nurse will help elevate the nursing department. The goal is a fully engaged nursing workforce. In addition, the Wright Model of Competency Assessment encourages unit innovation and creativity, which in itself is educational.

What Key Stakeholders Most Appreciated about the Model

- The model provides a better assessment of true competency than our previous process.

- The conversation between the leaders and staff to identify competency needs is valuable.

- The framework is consistent but flexible enough that it can be tailored to the unit.

- The model makes sense; it's practical and down to earth.

- Managers appreciated the setting of clear expectations and defining accountabilities.

- All nurse leaders and Human Resources came together to determine consequences for those who are not engaged—this will lead to consistency throughout the nursing department.

- The model encourages staff to seek out nurse leaders if they have questions; these conversations can foster critical thinking.

- The model uses adult learning principles such as giving staff members choices of ways to demonstrate competency, including evidence of daily work/practice.

After the decision was made to adopt the Wright Competency Model, Donna came back and met with the nursing leaders and conducted a workshop for the clinical nurse educators, which was very helpful.

Overcoming Our Most Difficult Competency Hurdles

The Wright Competency Model is very different from our previous process, and not everyone was sure the process would work. We are still working to change the culture and mindset about accountability, shifting it from the nurse leader to the staff. One hurdle was taking corrective action with those who were disengaged.

One hurdle was taking corrective action with those who were disengaged.

There is a certain amount of up-front work to develop the competency validation methods. Tools and templates were developed to assist with this.

Benefits to Individuals and the Organization

This year is the first full year in which all nursing units will be using the Wright Competency Model. Benefits recognized to date include:

- A common language/structure for the nursing department

- Use of adult learning principles

- Measuring/validating competence rather than providing education
- Flexibility
- Clear identification of those who are not engaged
- Options for validating

Carla Borchardt, MS, RN, NE-BC
Director of Professional Practice and Magnet® Program Director
Avera McKennan Hospital & University Health Center

A Change in Competency Assessment Improves Staff Unity

University of Pennsylvania Health System
Philadelphia, Pennsylvania

This academic medical center took a deep look at its competency process and came away with a higher level of clarity than they'd ever expected. They learned that a competency assessment process that empowers people and holds them accountable can have a unifying effect on the staff and therefore on the culture of the entire organization.

Motivation for Changing Our Competency Assessment Process

Our competency assessment process had not been evaluated or revised in 10+ years, and we wanted to move toward a competency process that could work system-wide. It was needlessly confusing that each entity had a different process, and competency assessment policies were often inconsistent (even within a single entity). We also wanted to automate more of our competency program, putting as much of it as possible online. We were in the process of revising the clinical ladder program, job descriptions, and domains of nursing practice too, so it seemed logical to redesign our competency assessment process at the same time.

Where We Were and Where We Wanted to Go

Before we discovered the Wright Model of Competency Assessment, there was really no competency assessment oversight or coordination. As a result of this lack of coordination, competencies were not always tied to the organization's overall vision. Some competencies were also assigned without talking to the staff about what they felt was needed, so there was nothing to foster a sense among the staff that they had any real ownership of the process. Despite these factors, some units were doing well, but some units didn't know who to turn to for help. On these units, the competency assessment process was marred by the use of limited verification methods, skills fairs that seemed to many like a waste of time and resources, and the overuse of tests. Because so much data was collected in so many different ways, an effective way to share and use the data was never found.

Once we discovered the Wright Competency Model, a new vision began to form. We realized it would make a lot of sense to validate competency in the clinical setting as often as possible, using evidence of daily work. If we determined competencies within our shared governance structure, the staff's sense of ownership of the process would increase, so we worked out a system where the leadership would collaborate with staff to determine competencies. We also took a fresh look at what competencies could and should look like hospital-wide and/or system-wide. We determined that competencies should be outcome-focused and use multiple and creative verification methods that develop reflective practice, measure daily work, and develop critical thinking skills.

Once we had some consistency in how competency assessment was being handled, we realized we also had an opportunity to create a competency assessment process that could be in better alignment with our system-wide nursing competency policy. We opened lines of communication with regulatory, Human Resources, and risk management departments to get their input. We determined what sort of language to use and we used it consistently—competency vs. annual mandatory education, etc., and we assigned a point person at each hospital or other organization within the health system to guide the process. It was important to us to make our new competency assessment process one in which clear accountabilities were determined for all roles, and there were clear and consistent consequences for not being accountable.

What Key Stakeholders Most Appreciated about the Model

We really saw clinical nurses grow through this process. At first they wanted to be "fed" the information, but once they understood things better and got a taste of the empowerment in this process, they really stepped up. The thing that may have made the biggest difference is that they really liked having a say in making competency selections that were highly relevant to their practice. Taking this process to shared governance committees and offering choices in the selection of validation methods has been very unifying and empowering. Now, rather than "one more thing to do," competency assessment acts as a confidence builder, really giving people a sense of, "I know this."

One curious side benefit of the change is that it created a sense of inquiry with other disciplines. For example, our system-wide interprofessional Critical Care Committee is developing insulin guidelines with a competency assessment to be used in all of our critical care units throughout the health system to standardize practice. We're seeing other opportunities to share with similar units across the health system as well.

A sense of unity among the clinical nurses was supported by having the Competency Committee speak at unit committee meetings. They also consulted with nurse managers and unit educators/clinical nurse specialists. Throughout this process, some policy weaknesses were identified and addressed, and we have moved toward more standardization throughout our organization. It has also been a big bonus that nurse managers are more involved in the process than they were with skills fairs, because it is easier to keep staff accountable when the nurse manager is included.

> Now, rather than "one more thing to do," competency assessment acts as a confidence builder, really giving people a sense of, "I know this."

Overcoming Our Most Difficult Competency Hurdles

When undertaking a change as big as this one, there are always multiple questions to be answered:

- What are the regulatory implications?

- What documentation is needed, and should it be on paper or computer?

- Who needs education to make this work, and how will we figure out how to provide it?

- Is there a way to manage competency for greater consistency system-wide? If so, who owns the process?

- Can our current learning management system function for both assigning and reporting of each individual's competencies?

We had these questions and more to deal with, and finding answers meant lots of conversations, some new partnerships, and a fair amount of compromise.

I think that some of our competency hurdles were due to our shifting accountability to the employee. It took a lot to get their buy-in, and initially there was a bit of push back. That also meant that we had to be careful to keep things developmental rather than punitive when things didn't go smoothly.

Overall, the biggest hurdle may have simply been that it was a big change which involved a lot of people and had a lot of moving parts. Some people didn't want to let go of skills fairs and simulations. Some more senior staff members were fearful of the process, and there was a lot of start-up work for the unit educators/clinical nurse specialist. Because we have so many ongoing initiatives in place, we had some change fatigue to deal with.

Benefits to Individuals and the Organization

Since we redesigned our competency assessment process, local management is more engaged and therefore more capable of holding staff accountable. Clinical nurse engagement in the process has improved significantly because the clinical nurses can see that we value their opinions in this process. Staff find that the new competencies are more relevant to practice when they are asked to select them, based on the data, and using Donna Wright's prioritization guidelines (found in *The Ultimate Guide to Competency Assessment in Health Care* on pages 27-29) to help narrow down the selection. Because of the changes we made to accommodate different styles by allowing staff to choose the method of verification, attitudes have changed. We no longer have to chase staff around, prodding them to bring the evidence forward!

Christine Sites, MSN, RN
Nursing Professional Development Specialist
University of Pennsylvania Health System

Results and Outcomes

Billings Clinic

Billings, Montana

The team in the Ambulatory Telemetry/Step Down Unit at Billings Clinic documented a decrease of 68% in the incidence of patient falls after redefining their competency strategy. This group boldly stepped out of old patterns of spending lots of time and energy on modules, mandated education, and other competency processes, to develop the strategies that would truly impact outcomes—strategies grounded in the Wright Competency Assessment Model tenets of ownership, empowerment, and accountability.

Problem

Organizations spend a lot of energy on competencies and education in an effort to fix some problem or reverse an undesirable trend. However, there are times when all the time and energy spent on education has no impact on the problem. A common lament is, "We did the education or 'lined everyone up and checked them off' ... and it did not improve anything!"

For this reason, the Billings Clinic team were looking at the selection of their ongoing competencies. They chose to focus on patient falls, which was one of their problematic indicators. The team explored several ways to address patient falls through competency assessment; they decided that addressing this competency in the traditional way would probably deliver a traditional (i.e., disappointing) result: lots of activity and effort, with no significant reductions in falls. They realized that there were actually two problem areas to address: too many falls and a competency process that for many years and in many settings within the organization had proven to be ineffective at reducing falls.

Solution

The team on this unit took a wider view of the problem, focusing on more creative methodologies to reach their desired outcomes. They started with the Wright

Competency Assessment Model to guide their planning for change that would work better for staff and create better outcomes for the patients. Here are the steps they took:

Rethink the all-too-common automatic response of providing education, a mandatory module, or competency training as the solution to what are actually performance issues.

Re-evaluate whether education is really the best answer for the issue. Is a knowledge deficit or learning gap really the cause of the problem? Will a mandatory competency module fix this? This group owned the problem of too many falls and decided, based on their past use of online education modules on fall reduction with no significant reduction in fall numbers, that it was time to get creative!

Identify the right action to reach the goal.

Harness the creative energy of the team to design and carry out the plan.

Create a targeted competency approach to truly affect the outcome.

Respond with the most fitting intervention possible—one that addresses the problem in the most direct way and that is also a good fit for the team.

The team determined that the answer to how to reduce falls could be found by exploring the interaction among nurses, other clinicians, technicians, and patients in hospital rooms, rather than through interacting with scenarios and test questions on a computer screen. So they set up a physical space in which to explore the falls issue: a room where people could play out mock scenarios. As staff members came into the room, they were asked the outside-of-the-box question, "If you *wanted* your patient to fall, what would you do in this room?" Staff members messed up the room, leaving things where they didn't belong, etc. When they were done "setting the patient up to fall," they were asked, "Do you do any of these things in your daily work routine?" The most typical answer was, "I don't do all of them, but I do some of them. OMG!"

> *They set up a physical space in which to explore the falls issue: a room where people could play out mock scenarios.*

Looking at the problem differently opened the door for staff to gain new insights about our contributions to falls:

- I was hurried.

- I was multi-tasking.

- I was not being present.

RESULTS AND OUTCOMES

The team was able to discover, accept, and work with these insights because they had come to their *own* conclusions through their *own* process. The team's second focus—that of changing their approach to their competency process—also added to this success. They were able to have a stronger impact on the outcome by allow their competency process go beyond the traditional mandatory training.

Billings Clinic is a perfect example of using The Wright Competency Model to achieve results that can be sustained. When the team decided to address the issue of falls, rather than slapping on a quick fix education or competency event, they brought a discussion of this problem into their competency reflection process. The Wright Competency Model encourages ownership, empowerment, and accountability for outcomes. If the problem is in fact a competency issue, what type of competency assessment is needed? Is it a technical skill, a critical thinking skill, or an interpersonal skill? Is the problem about a lack of skill in carrying out the procedure? Or do people not know how to speak up when the procedure is going wrong? Does the culture of the organization make speaking up unsafe?

> *The team determined that the answer to how to reduce falls could be found by exploring the interaction among nurses, other clinicians, technicians, and patients in hospital rooms, rather than through interacting with scenarios and test questions on a computer screen.*

This unit took hold of this problem, examined it from multiple sides to really understand the issues, and took a team approach to applying a solution. Their examination revealed that their high rate of falls was not just due to a simple knowledge deficit, but that factors like disruptive and distractive environments and the lack of attention to how patient rooms really function may be contributing to falls. They chose a very creative and appropriate modality for validation and improvement that focused on critical thinking and problem solving right in their patient rooms. They used mock scenarios, group discussion, and several process frameworks. They made learning fun and engaging. The staff created the process, owned it, and carried it out; they take pride in their work and feel good about preventing falls.

Ownership, empowerment, and accountability are keys to competency success and improved outcomes. Other people cannot own the work or impose a competency and then expect the results to be stellar. Success comes from the passion and engagement of the group. When this energy grows organically within a team,

COMPETENCY ASSESSMENT FIELD GUIDE

amazing things happen. The Billings Clinic team is a shining example of how out-of-the-box thinking can generate extraordinary results.

Outcomes

In the five years preceding this team project, the unit's rate of patient falls was below the NDNQI national average for only two quarters. Since the implementation of the project in 2012, they have experienced seven quarters below the national average. Hines and Yu estimate a cost per hospitalization for patient falls of $33,894, and the number of preventable injuries in the United States for fiscal year 2007 of 193,566 falls (2009). The estimated cost per fall ranges from $1,019 to $4,235 per case, with a rate of 3.73 falls per 1,000 patient-days. By reducing falls by 68%, the Billings Clinic team not only created a safer environment for patients; they also directly impacted the bottom line of their organization! See **Figure B.3** below.

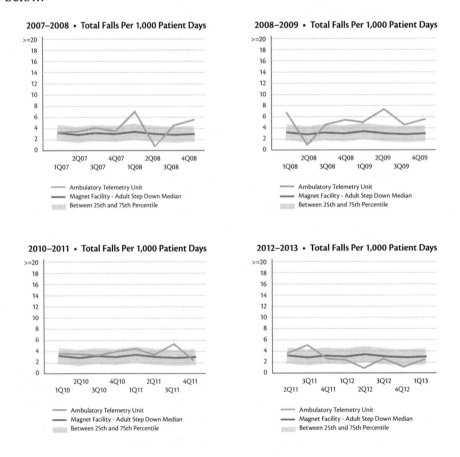

Figure B.3: Billings Clinic Falls Reduction Data

RESULTS AND OUTCOMES

Since realizing and sustaining these outstanding outcomes, staff members continue to identify and remove barriers, and Billings Clinic is rolling out the Wright Competency Model house-wide to use in other areas needing improvement.

Here's to the team at Billings Clinic!

Jennifer Tafelmeyer, BSN, RN, PCCN
Clinical Coordinator ATU

Laurie Smith, MSN, RN, CEN, CNML
Manager ATU

Robin Wicks, MSN, RN, PCCN
ATU Clinician
Billings Clinic

Fairfield Medical Center

Lancaster, Ohio

In 2010, Fairfield Medical Center (FMC) was surveyed by a prep team to prepare for an upcoming survey by The Joint Commission (TJC). One of the comments in the survey results humorously referred to our competency assessment process as "The Greatest Show on Earth." This comment referred to the much hyped, somewhat overblown annual skills fair conducted to evaluate the ability of FMC workers.

Problem

The competency assessment process gathered equipment into a central location, with checklists that addressed the technical use of the equipment. Each employee who used the equipment visited each station and had his or her list checked off by the evaluators. The Joint Commission surveyors pointed out that this method was good for assessing technical skills but did not address interpersonal relationships or the critical thinking skills of those using the equipment. These three domains of skill—technical, interpersonal, and critical thinking—had become industry standards in the 1980s based on the studies and writings of Dorothy del Bueno (del Bueno et. al, 1980).

The FMC Education Committee was tasked with evaluating "The Greatest Show on Earth" and making improvements in the competency assessment process at FMC. The committee members had no idea what a daunting task had been handed to them! We didn't know just how broken the process of evaluating competency was at our Center. We knew that improvements had to be made, and we wanted to assure that our employees were competent in doing their jobs and delivering the best possible care to our patients. We wanted to live up to the mission and vision set forth by Fairfield Medical Center, and our value statement, "PATIENTS FIRST" became the focus of the Education Committee.

Solution

Eventually "The Great Competency Make-Over" project outpaced the resources of the Education Committee, and the Competency Committee was born as a sub-group of the Education Committee in October, 2012. The sub-group focused solely on competency realignment; this distinction allowed the Education Committee to continue with its intended focus of coordinating educational events at FMC. I would strongly advise any facility that is considering changing their competency assessment process to have a dedicated group of people to facilitate those changes.

> *I would strongly advise any facility that is considering changing their competency assessment process to have a dedicated group of people to facilitate those changes.*

Implementation Phase 1: Review our Current Standards

The first thing the Competency Committee focused on was the many policies at FMC that addressed staff education. We asked each department to send us all their policies that dealt with staff education. The committee members reviewed and consolidated the key points of those policies. A major change that we made to these policies was to house all employee education policies in the Human Resources department (up to this time, individual departments were the "owners"). This created standardized expectations for every employee throughout the Center. It also helped to set the tone for the forthcoming changes in competency assessment.

Implementation Phase 2: Search the Literature

During the months that the Competency Committee was concentrating on policy round-up, the members of the committee were also searching for a new and improved competency assessment model. This process entailed educating our management team on the findings of TJC, reviewing policies and procedures that were already in place, conducting literature searches for best practices, reading books on competency assessment and reporting those ideas to the committee, and conducting a site visit to a hospital similar to ours. It was at this site visit that I discovered the Wright Competency Assessment Model. I was eager to meet with my manager and share the ideas from *The Ultimate Guide to Competency Assessment in Health Care*. My manager was already familiar with Donna Wright's concepts and gave her blessing to proceed in that direction. Our committee now had a concrete model on which to structure the new and improved FMC competency assessment process. We were psyched!

Implementation Phase 3: Adopt a Model for Competency Evaluation Improvement

The Competency Committee is composed of employees from all ranks and job descriptions, which makes for an enthusiastic and thought-provoking group. After months of search and discussion, our team chose the competency assessment principles of Donna Wright (2005), Patricia Benner (2001), and Dorothy del Bueno (1980, 1990). We ordered copies of Donna Wright's book, and all committee members read it. We wrote a synopsis of the book chapters and created a slide presentation to introduce the new format for employee competencies to the Fairfield Medical Center leadership team.

Implementation Phase 4: Divide the Investigative Work

At this point the project got a little off track. The team created four organizational competency measures that focused on assessment, actions/interventions, customer advocacy, and resource management. We had planned to use these as our competency assessment tools, but changed direction after a conference call with Donna Wright six months later. The tenet of the competency assessment model that our team had missed was the idea that the people in each job position need to choose their own competencies. Up to the time of our conference call with Donna, the committee had taken total ownership of the process: we had planned to create and hand out the competencies. I would strongly suggest that any organization that is planning to use the Wright Competency Assessment Model should have a conversation with Donna at the beginning of the transition. Our group worked for months going down the wrong road. We were able to change direction, but we lost a lot of time. We eventually abandoned this structure, but it did help us lay the groundwork for the department competency format that we finally adopted.

> *I would strongly suggest that any organization that is planning to use the Wright Competency Assessment Model should have a conversation with Donna at the beginning of the transition.*

Implementation Phase 5: Conduct an Assessment Survey of Current FMC Evaluation Model

Phase 4 and Phase 5 were happening at the same time. Mike Tobin, our committee representative from Six Sigma, conducted an on-line survey of the FMC leadership team. The results indicated that many managers still considered tasks to be the basis of competency. The committee realized that we had a lot of work to do in changing the ideology that the task is the skill, and to convince people that there is more to competency than performing the skill.

Implementation Phase 6: Create our New FMC Model

After the Competency Committee members finished our phone conference with Donna Wright, we knew we had to adjust our thinking from using competencies generated by leadership to competencies chosen and owned by the employees in each departmental job position. The committee members rallied and took a new direction; we held a workshop to size up what we had done and how we were going to change directions. It was at this workshop that we chose the title "Journey to Competency" and chose our logo photo. This task was fun; it gave the committee members a sense of ownership and a new road to travel. It also revitalized a committee that had come to a crossroads!

We created a communication timeline that included information emailed to leadership, articles for all employees in the in-house weekly newspaper *Monday Morning,* and invitations to attend Donna Wright workshops scheduled for the following February.

Here is the announcement that appeared in the *Monday Morning* after Donna's visit to FMC:

The FMC Competency Committee hosted Donna Wright, consultant for Creative Health Care Management and author of the book *The Ultimate Guide to Competency Assessment in Health Care.* Donna delivered her message on competency and validation methods to sessions for leadership, employees, and the TDR department. Donna's message emphasizes that competency must reach beyond skill validation and checklists. Competency encompasses technical skills, critical thinking, and interpersonal relationships. The committee had adopted the theme "Journey to Competency" and the assembly rooms were transformed with a collection of travel memorabilia. Our message was: Every FMC employee will travel with us to make this new assessment model a success. You will be hearing more about this initiative over the next few months. Watch for upcoming announcements and join the fun as we roll out the new competency evaluation model.

RESULTS AND OUTCOMES

Figure B.4: Donna Wright Presenting at Fairfield Medical Center

Outcomes

Implementation Phase 7: Conduct Pilots in Three Departments to Begin Collecting Data

After Donna's visit to FMC, the committee began creating the timeline for rollout, and decided to conduct pilots to trial the processes and paperwork. Three departments agreed to conduct pilots for the competency model change: Contracts & Collections, PCU, and Surgery Pavilion. This explanation was presented to each of the units:

Introduction

Evidence-based practice demands that competency evaluation be assessed using the trilogy of knowledge: critical thinking, technical skills, and attitude (interpersonal relations). This pilot will demonstrate the use of the new Fairfield Medical Center (FMC) Competency Model by implementing the competency process in three departments (Contracts & Collections, PCU, and Surgery Pavilion).

Purpose of Pilot

Initiate the new FMC Competency model in three departments to explore the process of introducing, developing, and evaluating competencies for various job positions in those departments.

Objectives for Unit

Engage each employee in the process of choosing, performing, and verifying competencies for his or her job position.

Success of the pilots was evaluated using the following table.

Outcomes of Competency Assessment Pilots on Three Units		
Department and Leaders	**Methods**	**Results**
Contracts & Collections Off-site, non-clinical department located in Kroger Shopping Center in Lancaster. 34 employees in 9 different job positions. All employees expected to participate. **Manager:** Sharon Scruggs **Pilot coordinator:** Jamie Hurst **Committee chair:** Mary Rogers	**Interventions** Initial meeting April, 2013, in manager's office with Sharon Scruggs, Jamie Hurst, Mary Rogers, and committee member Laura Garrett in attendance. **Department Competency Team** chosen by leadership ability displayed by the employees.	**Engagement** Manager: High. Weekly reminders sent to employees—email and verbal communication. Educator: Department doesn't have one. Pilot coordinator: High. Overwhelmed at first, tremendous growth as pilot went on. Governance Team: Medium. Employees: All employees participated.

RESULTS AND OUTCOMES

\\	\\ Outcomes of Competency Assessment Pilots on Three Units	\\
Department and Leaders	**Methods**	**Results**
PCU Clinical department located in the hospital. 48 employees in 7 different job positions. All employees expected to participate. **Manager:** Carol Stefaniak **Educator/Pilot coordinator:** Deb Price	**Interventions** **Governance Committee** chosen by volunteering.	**Engagement** Manager: High. Weekly reminders via Friday Updates and CC Information Educator/Pilot coordinator: High. Governance Team: Medium **What have we learned?** Educator: Be certain there is an overall level of expectation for each competency we make in the future. Difficult to come up with competencies that were specific enough to prove.
Surgery Pavilion Clinical department located in the hospital. 19 employees in 8 different job positions. All employees expected to participate. **Assistant manager:** Joyce Lewis **Educator:** Laura Garrett **Pilot coordinators:** Laura Garrett & Becky Murray	**Interventions** Initial meeting in May with Joyce Lewis, Becky Murray and Laura Garrett, in attendance. **Model introduced** at unit meeting via PowerPoint and discussion by Laura & Becky. **Governance Committee** chosen by volunteering and appointment. Several flyers, meetings, and Q&A session to help staff identify verification methods. Competency Presentation Day August 29, 2013. 16 of the 19 staff members attended. Staff completed posters, crossword puzzles, and quizzes to demonstrate competency.	**Engagement** Manager: Medium. Reminders were sent to employees. Educator: High Pilot coordinators: High Governance Team: Medium Employees: At first discussion, said they were confused due to being a new process. Unsure about what they had to do to demonstrate competency and worried they would not have enough time to complete it. **What have we learned?** Staff: Verbalized that they learned about various surgical topics that were high-risk and low-volume. The educator felt need for more specific verification methods, e.g. more examples, verification by demonstration of work.

Figure B.5: Summary of Outcomes of Competency Assessment Pilots on Three Units

Implementation Phase 8: Introduce FMC Model to Management Team

Getting the leadership team on board had been an ongoing process. Over an 18-month period, the members of the Competency Committee took information from our meetings back to their departments. I made an appearance at the mangers' meeting and announced the findings of TJC and that changes in competency assessment were coming. Articles appeared in *Monday Morning*. All leadership personnel were personally invited to attend Donna Wright's leadership presentation.

After Donna's visit, all members of the leadership team were invited to attend one of the six showings of the videotape of Donna's presentation to the FMC staff. DVDs were made available for any leader who wasn't able to attend the planned sessions. These were fun sessions, with a popcorn machine and boxes of movie candy for those attending the film.

Implementation Phase 9: Introduce FMC Model to Employees

The employee rollout has been accomplished through communications similar to those offered to management. Articles have appeared in *Monday Morning*. Currently, I am conducting "Journey to Competency" coaching sessions that outline the new process for competency evaluation that will go into effect next. I use a slide presentation and also show a video clip of Donna's presentation of the verification methods.

The biggest hurdle encountered has been the timeline. There are so many changes in health care and the requirements for hospitals (e.g., Meaningful Use) that the timeline for the competency change rollout has been pushed back several times. As of this writing, I am waiting for the go-ahead to announce the changes. I feel that many people in our organization are already aware of the coming changes to our competency process and are preparing for the change.

Mary Rogers, MSN, RN, CNOR
Clinical Education Coordinator
Fairfield Medical Center

Arkansas Children's Hospital

Little Rock, Arkansas

Problem

At Arkansas Children's Hospital, nursing competencies were defined as nearly any information that needed to reach the masses, usually in a short amount of time. The process was not evidence-based, and it lacked both rationale and data to support the need for specific competencies. The educators identified the lack of comprehensive competency assessment at the unit level and challenged the nurse leaders to take more ownership and accountability for the competency assessment process.

The key drivers for adopting the Wright Competency Assessment Model were complexity compression and the need for a consistent approach. There were so many competencies and education initiatives that it was difficult for individuals to manage, comprehend, and retain everything. Not only did the competencies seem random; they were often irrelevant and/or poorly planned and communicated. During one six-week period, sixteen new mandatory initiatives/competencies were rolled out for staff to complete.

In addition to complexity compression, competency education was inconsistent within the organization. Each unit had its own interpretation of what was required, making managing and tracking the process extremely difficult for central educators. Lack of compliance with regulatory requirements for education was a major concern.

> *The key drivers for adopting the Wright Competency Assessment Model were complexity compression and the need for a consistent approach.*

Our competency assessment process had been the same for so long that even though it wasn't working, the staff were comfortable with it and didn't want to change. Every action, every skill had an associated competency. Whenever a problem occurred, mandatory education was the answer. There was no systematic process for rolling out education initiatives. Often, new policies and procedures

COMPETENCY ASSESSMENT FIELD GUIDE

> *Whenever a problem occurred, mandatory education was the answer.*

were approved without any education and pushed out to staff with an unreasonable deadline.

We needed a new process for managing annual competency assessment while prioritizing new education initiatives throughout the year. The new process needed to address the complexity compression that nurses were experiencing, while also fostering staff compliance by demonstrating that standardizing and prioritizing education would have a positive impact on patient outcomes.

Solution

Patient safety is the number one strategic goal for the hospital, and the educators agreed that education and competencies that impact safety (e.g. medication administration) must receive top priority. Next priorities were patient/family impact, staff-identified needs, and ancillary department requests. The 2013 Annual Central Education and Competency initiative was a deliberate, planned dissemination comprising quarterly rollouts of these prioritized education initiatives, each with an education plan with identified outcomes.

The Wright Competency Assessment Model was integrated into the organization's framework for education and professional development which included "competence program" as one of the throughputs for achieving nursing professional excellence. See **Figure B.6** on the following page.

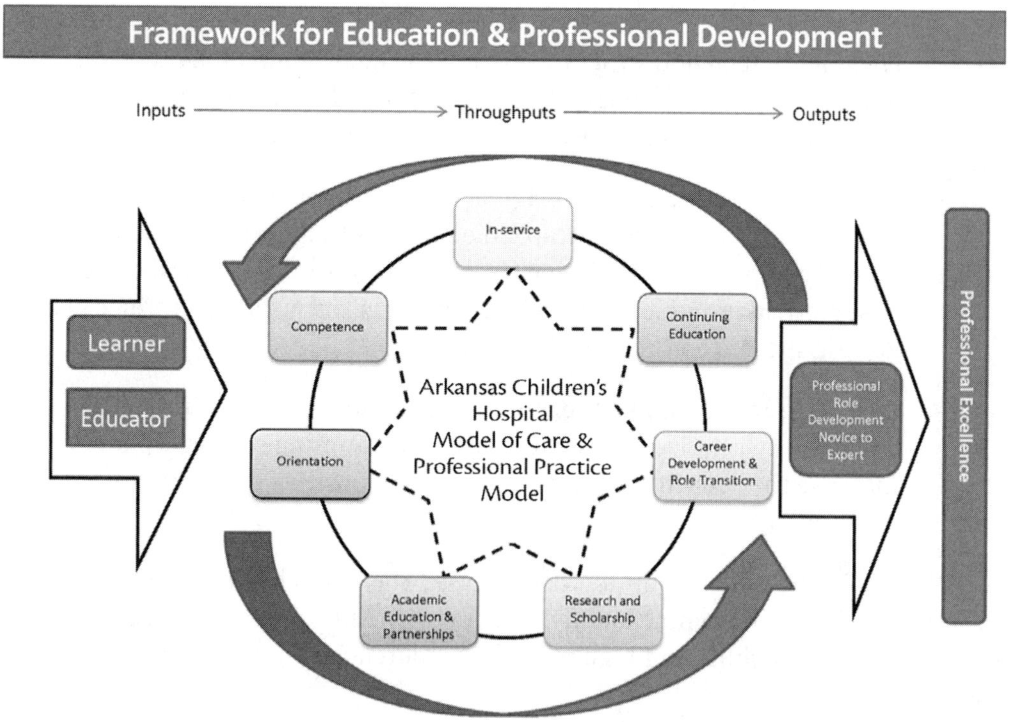

RESULTS AND OUTCOMES

Framework for Education & Professional Development

Inputs → Throughputs → Outputs

Learner / Educator → [In-service, Competence, Continuing Education, Orientation, Career Development & Role Transition, Academic Education & Partnerships, Research and Scholarship] around *Arkansas Children's Hospital Model of Care & Professional Practice Model* → Professional Role Development Novice to Expert → Professional Excellence

Figure B.6: Arkansas Children's Hospital: A Framework for Education and Professional Development (Webb & Walker, 2012, used with permission)

Framework for Education and Professional Development

Implementation of the Wright Competency Assessment Model enabled the educators to operationalize the framework, which improved awareness, understanding, and performance.

- Staff: Staff's perception of the value of a competency program improved with the increased participation in the development and awareness of the rationale for selection of the specific competencies. Nurses felt respected and valued because their concerns were addressed and the program met their needs.

- Managers: Gained new understanding of the need for and value of a competency assessment process. The nurse managers can utilize this program to attain positive quality outcomes for their departmental goals.

- Unit-based Educators: Benefited from the collaboration and partnership with the central educators to assist in the facilitation of decision making with the departmental leadership and staff, which helped to gain buy in, support, and additional resources.

- Centralized Educators: The original design provided a framework for the master's-prepared centralized educators to define the centralized annual competency requirements, rationale for inclusion, risks of skill, best method for education, and alignment to the nursing strategic plan. See **Figure B.6** on the previous page.

- Executive Team: Gained the ability to align the identified annual competency requirements with the overall nursing strategic plan to increase the capacity to obtain and sustain positive outcomes for nursing performance and patient outcomes.

When meeting with the units, we discussed the new, changing, high-risk, and problematic areas for each department. It was difficult to persuade some areas to eliminate high-risk skills and high volume competencies that were not supported by data.

The process of meeting with each unit individually was time-consuming for the centralized educators as well as for nurse leaders; however, the Worksheet for Identifying Competencies and Annual Training from Donna Wright's book (*The Ultimate Guide to Competency Assessment in Health Care,* pages 25-26) provided the clarity and direction needed to engage the teams in the process. At the unit level, issues encountered included participation and buy-in from nurse leaders and staff, understanding the rationale for the education and competencies selected, and obtaining up-to-date quality data.

> *Our biggest obstacle was trying to explain the difference between education deficits and accountability issues.*

Our biggest obstacle was trying to explain the difference between education deficits and accountability issues. Convincing unit and organizational leaders that some issues were actually accountability issues rather than education deficits was challenging. Through our newly developed Educator Council, the central and unit-based educators developed the following algorithm to help identify education/competence/compliance for each new educational request or initiative. See **Figure B.7** on the following page.

RESULTS AND OUTCOMES

Arkansas Children's Hospital Education Initiative Evaluation

I. Determine the need for training and education:
1. Assess the need for change through training and education › Who is bringing this forward (groups/individual)? › What is the change or training/education that is needed? › What is the desired change/outcome of the training/education?
2. Determine background information. › Why is this being brought forward? › What are the driving forces for the change? (QI, regulatory, competency, NPSG, etc.) › What is the evidence (internal or external) that training/education resulting in change is needed? Is additional information/evidence needed?
3. Identify the stakeholders. › Who needs the training/education? › Who will be affected by the change as a result of the training/education? › Who are the key groups to be involved?
4. Identify existing resources. › Identify any information relative to the training/education, policy/procedures, learning modules, training system). › Are there similar training/education activities, courses, etc., that already exist externally? › Identify any other groups which may be working on a similar project.
5. Determine the issue. › Is this a training/education need or an accountability/compliance issue? › Are there policy/procedures in place which are not followed? › Are there alternative solutions? › For compliance issues – Assess accountability. Who will address? › For education needs – An education plan is needed.

II. Prepare an Education Plan. An education plan should answer:

- › Who are/will be the content experts?
- › Who is developing the actual education content?
- › Who will provide the training?
- › Who will be trained?
- › Will super users be appointed?
- › What are the education methods and teaching strategies being used?
- › Who will review the education content prior to the roll out?
- › What is the timetable?
- › How will the learning be measured?
- › How will the change be measured?
- › Are there other outcomes?

III. Evaluation Process for Education Initiative: Kirkpatrick's* Evaluation Model:

1. **Reaction/learner satisfaction:** To what degree participants react favorably to the learning event.

   Examples: Course evaluation, participant feedback, Q & A

2. **Learning/knowledge acquisition:** To what degree participants acquire the intended knowledge, skills, and attitude based on their participation in the learning event.

   Examples: pre/post test, competency verification, recall

3. **Behavior:** To what degree participants apply what they learned during training when they are back on the job.

   Examples: Audits, observation, return demonstration, peer review, interviews

4. **Results/impact:** To what degree targeted outcomes occur, as a result of the learning event and subsequent reinforcement.

   Examples: Nurse sensitive measures, patient satisfaction, performance indicators, costs, retention

* Donald Kirkpatrick's four level evaluation model is well known in education circles. It was initially published in 1959, then updated in 1975, and again in 1994.

Figure B.7: Arkansas Children's Hospital Education Initiative Evaluation

Outcomes

Overcoming these hurdles led to the revision of our Nursing Competency Policy, reinforcing accountability and quarterly compliance as a professional performance standard. The dream goals that our organization realized thus far include:

Increased patient safety and improved patient outcomes, including a significant reduction in overall infection rates. Through the process of selecting evidence-based competencies, new bundles were implemented, followed by lower rates of urinary tract infections (UTIs) and central venous line-associated infections. We remain well below the benchmark we set for hospital-associated infection rates since implementation of the new competencies in 2011, and are currently outperforming external benchmarks for ICU central-line-associated bloodstream infections and catheter-associated UTIs.

Prioritization of education throughout the year and decreased education costs and staff hours allocated for education and assessment of required competencies. The medical surgical units reported an 80% reduction in education costs after implementation of the model.

Increased staff satisfaction and compliance with completing education requirements, due in large part to manageable, unit-based shared decision making on competency development. This has reduced nurses' perception of complexity compression and increased professional accountability, as evidenced by 100% completion of all annual competency and education requirements.

Consistent communication, increased frontline collaboration, and standardization of practice are other significant benefits recognized by changing to the Wright Competency Assessment Model, including improved overall teamwork among educators, nurse leaders, and direct care nurses, and a consistent process to identify what is and what is not a competency.

Tammy Webb, MS, RN, NE-BC
Vice President Acute Care

Julie Bane, MS, RN-BC
Clinical Education Specialist

Barbara Johns, MHA, BSN, RN
Clinical Education Specialist

Felisha Mason, MSN, RN, CPN
Clinical Education Specialist

Lametria Wafford, MNSc, RN-BC
Clinical Education Specialist
Arkansas Children's Hospital

Charles George Veterans Affairs Medical Center

Asheville, North Carolina

Problem

At Charles George Veterans Affairs Medical Center, we knew we needed a way to assure competency. Our formal competency assessment process was a meaningless task: it was repetitive, checklist-based, and not respected by the staff. Our actual competency assessment was informal, hit-and-miss, and preceptor-driven.

The Charles George nursing staff has always recognized the importance of assuring initial and ongoing competency. New staff are constantly scrutinized for competence by their peers, but on an informal basis.

On the surface, finding competence seems simple. Everyone can identify the "go-to" staff members who are respected for their competence. "Matt has great skill but also the knowledge. When things don't go well he can trouble-shoot. Plus, he is so kind and tries so hard." Competence is not hard to spot, but measuring and documenting it proves complicated. The sheer number of skills, the volume of knowledge, and the difficulty of quantifying attitude all add to the complexity. At our hospital, new staff members did get assessed, but the assessment was driven by the individual preceptor and was certainly hit-and-miss. The pencil-and-paper checklists bore no relation to the real assessment; they only served as a reminder to cover all the bases, and often did not get done.

> *Competence is not hard to spot, but measuring and documenting it proves complicated.*

Competencies only got attention when survey teams were due to arrive. This meant sleepless nights struggling to obtain the correct forms, get signatures, and assure that we had no unmanageably long lines of staff members waiting to do their competencies. Nurse mangers fought with educators, educators blamed nurse mangers, and a positive outcome was achieved only by pure luck if the surveyors happened to pick a folder that was complete. Everyone complained about the reactive approach and swore that next year would be better, but it never was.

Over the years we tried various methods to improve. One involved developing a rubric of exemplar statements on a novice-to-expert scale using appreciative inquiry and interviewing to determine level of competency. This system earned us several awards for innovation, and national recognition. There was just one problem: managers could not use the tool properly. It required a high level of interviewing skill, took considerable time, and demanded an ability to confront and give feedback. After years of trying to make it work, we had to recognize its limitations.

We lacked a meaningful and respected process, doable with our current resources, with the employee at the center. One staff member wrote in response to the question of where we wanted to go: "A world in which practitioners embrace the concept of ongoing professional development, a world in which they show interest in and even enthusiasm for seeking knowledge in order to engineer not only their own growth, but that of their colleagues; and, a world in which they accept responsibility for pursuing such knowledge and are eager to share their knowledge and skills with others. Finally, I dream of a world in which such a person would be welcomed and appreciated."

Solution

As the Wright Competency Model recommends, we started by developing ongoing competencies, even though many wanted to start with new employee competencies. I am very glad we used this approach because when we did move on to tackle our initial and position-specific competencies, we were quickly overwhelmed with the volume of content. If we had started with the initial and position-specific competencies, I think we would have given up.

The hardest part was remembering to keep the staff at the center. For the basic or core content, we initially made the mistake of limiting the verification method to evidence of daily practice. The staff were not at the center in choosing a verification method. We found that the process quickly became a check sheet with the preceptors or educators flying down the list—more of a teaching tool than a verification.

We began our position-specific competencies by asking the staff to choose a verification method for each item; this proved unworkable due to the volume of information that has to be covered. Our solution was to group the items (safety, programs and services, equipment, documentation, communication, and philosophy) and ask the new staff to choose verification methods in each of the three areas: skills, knowledge, and attitude. New staff will create a portfolio and hand it in at the end of orientation. Orienters, especially in critical care, are struggling with not having a verification method for every single item identified. We ask them to look at the quality of the submitted portfolio and see if they can infer whether the person can be deemed competent. The big-picture people are much more comfortable with this approach, but the detail-oriented people are struggling. We point out that having the staff do 250 skill check sheets (the actual number of critical care skills required) would make the system unmanageable. We have developed companion resource manuals to outline all specifics of each skill, and this helps the detail-oriented people who want to know the exact content. One of the first things our staff appreciated was the relevance of the competency items. Our new assessment process assured that the items were specific to clinical areas, and there was an appreciation that the items really did matter. For example, one item chosen for a core safety competency was use of the emergency Evacusleds® (equipment for getting mattresses down the stairwell in an emergency). Many staff said, "I didn't know about this. This is important for me to know." This created an eagerness and appreciation for the content.

The staff really appreciated not having to do the same topics over and over. We have benefitted from Donna Wright's insight about how we are often responsible for creating our own competency headaches. For example, we used to hound all the staff to be signed off in demonstrating the use of leather restraints every year. What a battle! Then we discovered that regulations did not mandate yearly demonstrations, but said we must have systems in place to assure correct application and incorporate restraints into our overall competency process. We

> *We have benefitted from Donna Wright's insight about how we are often responsible for creating our own competency headaches.*

had previously made the decision that demonstrations would be done yearly on all units. Now we are clear that each unit will monitor their quality indicators and address restraint application if needed. Our inpatient mental health unit got a new type of restraint, and they answer crisis calls. Therefore they chose restraints as an ongoing competency for that year. This made perfect sense as it was a new product, the concern was time-sensitive, and the circumstances high-risk.

Staff members appreciate having multiple methods for verification and being able to choose one that works best for them. One verification method was to conduct a short in-service for another service; another choice was writing a one-page paper. A staff member told me, "Oh, I love teaching and having an audience. That would be easy for me, but writing a paper would be hell." The very next staff member said to me, "Getting up in front of people would be hell for me, but I am in school and I am writing up things all the time—how easy!"

We still have staff members who resist and wait till the last minute, but many of our staff now appreciate the structure and clarity of the process. They like getting work done and demonstrating their care. We had not fully appreciated the number of staff who take pride in showing their work. It gives them a platform. For example, our primary care unit is working hard to increase the care management skills of the RNs. This expectation is new for them, and they chose it as an ongoing competency. One verification method was to write up a case in which the nurse was actively involved. This called for an exemplar. The following is an example that clearly demonstrates the skill, knowledge, and attitude needed to manage care with finesse as expressed in the employee's exemplar.

> *Staff members appreciate having multiple methods for verification and being able to choose one that works best for them.*

Exemplar Written by an RN at the VA: Example of Demonstrating Assessment and Critical Thinking in this Role

Care Management of a Specific Population

I worked with a veteran in care management of his health, focusing mainly on his hypertension, diabetes, and medication management. Mr. S. was frequently viewed as "non-compliant" and had many complaints of not feeling well, with multiple vague health concerns. He had frequent walk-in clinic nurse appointments, emergency department visits, and hospital admissions. He had a CAN (care assessment need) score of 99, which is my current focus in care management.

Mr. S. was admitted to VA for hypertension and had medication changes. Three days later I saw Mr. S. in a walk-in nurse appointment. Blood pressure was elevated 208/113, 206/109, HR 81. As on previous visits and in conversations, he was vague about his symptoms and health management. He was lethargic and did not participate much in discussion of his health care. I discussed Care Coordination Home Telehealth (CCHT) and sent a consult to help him manage his diabetes and hypertension; however he did not return contact so the consult was discontinued. I spoke with Social Services to see if home health was available to assess his home environment and assist with medications, but it was not available to him through VA.

Mr. S. and I decided that the best plan was for him to see me in nurse clinic once a week to review his meds and home blood pressure (BP) and blood sugar (BS) readings and to fill his pill box. I created a daily medication, BP, and BS log that included the best times for him to take his medications (he would forget afternoon meds and would fall asleep before taking evening meds). We discussed setting alarms to help him remember his meds. We talked at length about the importance of medication management and how if he were more involved and compliant he may be able to decrease the amount of meds he had to take, which was an important goal for him.

Six days later he was admitted for hypertension and was prescribed different hypertension medications, which confused him. I obtained the records from his admission and his primary physician developed a medication plan for him. We discussed the importance of knowing his medications and informing all his providers about them.

Mr. S. and I continued weekly visits. He was becoming more compliant with medications; the pill box showed that most medications were being taken. His BP was improving. BS was still fluctuating and we talked about managing his diabetes better. He was well educated on proper diet but non-compliant. I offered diabetes education with a dietician and/or diabetes nurse, but he declined, stating that he was aware of what he needed to do but was not ready at that time.

I ordered a basket for his scooter to help him carry items, and a new cane to assist with ambulation, as he had lost his a long time ago. I noticed that he felt uncomfortable taking his BP at home. I obtained a new home BP monitor; at each visit he took his BP with his home monitor and then I would take my readings. This helped him feel more confident that he was taking his BP correctly at home.

Mr. S. was gradually becoming more alert; he reported that he felt better and had more energy. He started to really open up to me; he had a wonderful, funny personality. He had a lot of interesting life experiences and enjoyed sharing them with staff. I discovered that he had been a musician all his life, and he enjoyed sharing his love of music and other parts of his life history.

Eventually we decided that he could see me every 2 weeks; I obtained another pill box and we would fill 2 pill boxes at each visit. His BP continued to improve and he would always report that he felt so much better.

Mr. S. used an electric scooter and I started helping him to his car after visits. I never realized how difficult traveling and transporting his scooter was for him. He had difficulty walking and was very unsteady. I was concerned for his safety in traveling to the VA and explained VA home-based primary care to him. He was interested in this, so I sent a consult and he was enrolled with them in the next week.

Working with Mr. S. really helped open my eyes to how poor health can affect a person, and how having someone take an interest in them and their health can help them start to care about managing their own health better. Once Mr. S. started to feel better, he was able to really show his personality and the person he is, and that was great to see.

Outcomes

In general, nurse managers appreciate the simplicity and effectiveness of the new model. Their comments include: "More validation to hold people accountable;" "Makes it easier to address issues with staff;" "More confidence in the process;" "Makes it easier to determine what is a competency and what it means to validate;" "Decreased misinterpretation."

We are on year four, and many managers are expressing gratitude for the timeliness of the completion of the competencies. We meet monthly with a group that includes nursing representation from every unit. We communicate percentages completed with the nurse managers. Some managers are better cheerleaders than others, but the expectation is slowly creeping into our culture.

It is easy to see that the process is fluid as we adapt the model to meet our needs. We have committed to managing the program with a professional development council of bedside nurses from each unit. The council meets monthly, and we strive for consensus in making decisions on how to proceed. Often we have to return to the principals of Donna's work when we get lost (for example, keeping the staff at the center of the process). Consensus decision making is slow and at times frustrating, but it has created a level of engagement and buy-in that we have never had before.

> *Consensus decision making is slow and at times frustrating, but it has created a level of engagement and buy-in that we have never had before.*

We are now better prepared for surveys, but the larger benefit is enhanced quality of care. The Emergency Department (ED) staff writes, "One of our competencies was treating acquired angioedema. We had a vet come to the ED with this condition, and he was treated appropriately. Nurses knew about the drugs and treatments."

The process unearths concerns and gives opportunities for teaching and supporting the staff. One example was submitted by a staff member in the inpatient mental health unit. The competency concerned managing violent behavior of veterans in time of crisis. This staff member chose to write an exemplar of a violent situation. In reading his work it became clear that he was struggling with control/domination issues. The nurse manager and educator were able to work with him and give him future strategies to better cope in these situations. The exemplar was able to lift up this need to help the employee develop to a more effective level of care delivery and response.

In another example, the long-term care unit was working on increasing accuracy in weighing patients. One verification method was to weigh one person using the sling, the standing scale, and the wheelchair scale. Several patients had discrepancies between the wheelchair weight and the standing weight. Sure enough, those staff members were not subtracting the weight of the wheel chair. No wonder weights were incorrect. This model let us zero in on the decision making and attitude (task-centered), and pinpoint the education needed.

Finally, another benefit for us has been our willingness to tackle another innovation: managing our competencies on the computer rather than with pen and paper. Donna's emphasis on making the process real and manageable led us to convert the forms to fillable PDFs which are saved on a network drive. We credit Donna Wright's model for providing us with the theoretical framework to succeed.

Kitty Hancock, MSN, RN
Nurse Educator
Charles George Veterans Affairs Medical Center

Baptist Health South Florida

Miami, Florida

Problem

Competency is a requirement for all nurses to ensure that safe, quality care is provided to the clientele. For years, Baptist Health South Florida has used annual or semi-annual skills fairs to assess nurses' competency; our assessment model was process-oriented, not focused on outcomes.

Managers and unit educators met yearly to decide what needed to be included in the annual competency assessment for each unit or area. Criteria included changes anticipated in the near future, problems that had occurred in one or two areas, and some skills that are performed by all nurses.

The skills fair was facilitated by the nurse educators and was mandatory for all nurses. Nurses spent 8 to 12 hours of paid time away from their units completing skills stations manned by the educators and staff from other departments (e.g., risk management, infection control, patient satisfaction, and core measures).

Solution

The BHSF Patient Care Leadership Council, composed of the chief nursing officers of all the entities, set a two-year goal of transitioning all nurse competency assessment to the Wright Competency Model. This would empower the nursing staff to have control over their professional practice.

In addition to staff empowerment, the accountability of individual staff nurses for their own competency is a strong benefit. The model promotes critical thinking and incorporates adult learning principles, giving the staff the opportunity to choose how their competencies are verified. It promotes teamwork (nurses communicate with and help each other) and individual learning (nurses are able to review high-risk, low-volume, time-sensitive interventions on their own). The unit-based competencies are relevant to each nurse's specific practice.

Effective competency assessment happens at the bedside. As Donna Wright said in her presentation to BHSF, competency assessment done in the classroom allows the nurse to incur "safe errors." When the nurse leaves the practice setting for a classroom and then is given a scenario, an incorrect or inappropriate response can be readdressed until the nurse gets it right, which does not happen with real patients.

> *The model promotes critical thinking and incorporates adult learning principles, giving the staff the opportunity to choose how their competencies are verified.*

From the leadership perspective, the model serves as a needs assessment and allows for budgetary variance. For organizations pursuing Magnet® designation, the model addresses aspects of the forces of magnetism:

Force #5: Nurses are accountable for their own practice as well as the coordination of care.

Force #9: Autonomous nursing care is the ability of a nurse to assess and provide nursing actions as appropriate for patient care based on competence, professional expertise and knowledge.

Searching the Literature

According to Dorothy del Bueno (1990), competency assessment is the effective application of knowledge and skills in the work setting. Benner (1982) defines competency as the ability to perform a task with desirable outcomes under the varied circumstances of the real world. With these definitions, the Clinical Learning department began a study of how competency assessment can be meaningful to nurses and ensure the public of safe practice.

The query on competency assessment began with an extensive literature search, which yielded a broad discussion but not a clear, concise map of competency, due to varied definitions of the concept. There is ample literature on competency, with a united understanding of its importance, but not of the processes involved.

Clinical Learning consulted with Dr. Diana Swihart, who has deep interest in competency, especially in adapting the Wright Competency Model. It was Dr. Swihart who encouraged us to pursue the competency journey; she introduced us to Donna Wright and her model. We consulted with Donna, read her book on competency, and devised an implementation plan for our organization

Preparing to Pilot

After consulting with Donna to understand her model, we proceeded to solicit the sponsorship of a pilot implementation at one of our hospitals. Clinical Learning obtained approval from the Chief Nursing Officer and conducted a meeting with the nursing director of the medical/surgical units, the director of education, a representative from human resources, and the manager of the unit where the pilot would be implemented.

Information about the pilot was disseminated to the unit via flyers posted on the bulletin board, a staff meeting, and one-on-one meetings with staff members. Other necessary preparation included:

- Creating a shared drive for the unit so that staff can access all the forms and other information needed to complete the competency assessment in a timely manner.

- Designating a place in the unit where staff can keep their competency forms while they are in process. Having a designated place also facilitates follow-up of the staff's progress by leadership so that appropriate measures can be taken to ensure their completion in a timely manner.

- Writing the guidelines for the process of the unit-based competency assessment.

- Writing verification guidelines and a list of appropriate verifiers. (For example, nurses with pending clinical corrective action cannot verify competency of other staff; former nurse residents cannot verify competency of other staff unless progressed from novice or advanced beginner status to proficient nurses status; nurses who are new to the facility but have experience can be verifiers after six months of employment).

- Generating a template for a commitment letter, a document that explains the transition of the organization's competency assessment to a unit-based system. All parties (staff members, manager, and unit educator) sign this letter as a commitment to this journey.

- Generating a template for an accountability letter, a document approved by HR, signed by the nurses and provided to the manager in the event that a staff member does not comply with the unit-based competency assessment by the due date. If noncompliant, staff members are removed from the work schedule until competency has been established.

- Developing the education plan, including the roles of the manager, assistant nurse manager, patient care supervisors, and clinical nurse educator in the unit-based competency assessment system.

The initiative was presented to the unit practice council (UPC), and then to the whole staff in mandatory sessions over one month. The education consisted of two parts: theory and process, and specifics of the verification process, including role play of a case scenario.

Choosing Competencies

After the education, Clinical Learning representatives met with the UPC to solicit staff's input into the contents of the list of competencies. Clinical Learning reps compiled the input, then met with the UPC, nurse manager, and clinical nurse educator. In this meeting we decided on the ongoing unit competencies (what's new, been revised, high-risk, or problematic). The UPC chose the time frame for that cycle (annual or biennial) and provided input into the verification methods for each competency. Once the competencies were identified, the clinical nurse educator prepared the appropriate forms, which were then posted on the unit-based shared drive, where they are available to staff round the clock.

Rollout and Roles

Once all documents were created and competencies identified, the rollout started. During the cycle, the role of management (manager, assistant nurse manager, and patient care supervisors) is to remind the staff about the competency process and provide support to ensure a successful completion. Clinical Learning's role was to be the lead facilitator for the initiative, to be visible on the unit, to support the staff, and to offer clarification of the process if needed.

A month or two prior to the end of the cycle, the UPC convenes and identifies the next set of unit competencies. The day after the end of the cycle, the clinical nurse educator emails staff members who have not satisfactorily completed their competencies, cc'ing the manager who then sends the letter of accountability and removes the staff member from the work schedule until competency is established.

Outcomes

Results of Pilots

The pilot implementation was a success. The staff was surveyed anonymously about the pilot implementation of the competency process. Clinical Learning presented to hospital leadership about what worked, what did not work, and lessons learned.

Because of the success of the pilot implementation, the hospital leadership decided to conduct a second pilot in a bigger unit, implementing it across all disciplines. The same steps were done, adding guidelines to the verification process reflecting the different disciplines. This pilot was also very successful, leading to implementation of unit-based competency assessment for all disciplines in the hospital.

Moving Forward with Organization-wide Implementation

After the success of the pilots, the proposed transition to unit-based competency assessment using the Wright Competency Assessment Model was presented to the nursing leadership of BHSF's Patient Centered Leadership Council (PCLC), in order to obtain buy-in from top leadership and approval to proceed with implementation across the organization. After the presentation, Donna Wright was invited to address the leadership of Baptist Health about her model. The PCLC gave approval for system-wide implementation of the new model, with a two-year time frame.

Donna also presented a one-day seminar to the organization's clinical nurse educators to give them a clear understanding of the model. I followed up with a workshop for the clinical nurse educators. I also created a shared drive for them containing the following:

- Templates (competency forms, verification methods)
- Educational materials for the staff as the units roll out unit-based competency assessment
- Documents (UPC process guidelines, commitment letter, accountability letter)
- Finished competencies from different units as references for others
- Flyers

Clinical Learning created uniform educational materials to be used by all educators so that the same information is disseminated to all staff. We provided further education for staff when requested by the educators. During the two-year transition to the unit-based competency assessment, Clinical Learning acted as consultants to ensure that the process would be smooth.

Ongoing Process

The management team (managers, assistant nurse managers, and patient care supervisors) were concerned that some staff members could not be trusted to maintain the integrity of the validation process and would sign off on competencies without careful attention. The managers need to be involved in the sign-off process because it is part of the annual performance review.

Clinical Nurse Educators had similar concerns that staff "will just check each other off." Some educators felt that they needed to be part of the check-offs themselves, stating, "I need to check them off so that I know if they are truly competent." They felt a loss of control and wondered how staff would comply. Also, preparing all the documents needed was labor-intensive.

Some staff members shared the managers' and educators' concerns about the reliability of the validation process, thinking that friends would just sign each other off. Some did not like the idea of being accountable for their own competency, thinking that it is the responsibility of the educators. They wondered what the educators would do now. They also questioned whether they would have enough time to complete the process.

Continuous monitoring of the transition was accomplished through the clinical educators' forum.

By the end of the second year, the competency assessment for nurses had been transitioned to the unit-based system using Wright's model. Many units had transitioned other disciplines' competency assessments as well, including administrative secretaries, care partners, respiratory therapists, dieticians, radiology technicians, physical therapists, occupational therapists, and social workers.

A three-phase unit-based competency study approved by the Institutional Review Board (IRB) is ongoing. Clinical Learning has concluded the first phase, comparing skills fairs with unit-based competency from the perspective of the leaders and the staff. We are in the process of preparing the manuscript for this phase for publication. We are currently on phase two, creating the assessment tool for the implementation of the unit-based competency.

Solimar Figueroa, MSN, MHA, BSN, RN
Clinical Educator-Clinical Learning
Baptist Health South Florida

Sharp Memorial Hospital

San Diego, California

Problem

In today's economic health care climate of scarce resources, it is important to implement innovative methods to evaluate nursing competency and preserve limited education dollars. Sharp Memorial Hospital used a competency assessment model for validating annual competence, which included a significant amount of non-productive nursing time and education dollars and did not meet individual employee learning needs or unit/department resource demands.

Solution

Four progressive care units (PCUs) at Sharp Memorial Hospital replaced the traditional annual skills day for validating clinical competence with a diverse evaluation program that involved nurse-selected modalities as introduced by the Wright Competency Assessment Model. While the annual skills day had typically featured simulated clinical scenarios, the various verification methods used in the revised process included a written exam, return demonstration, evidence of daily work, case studies, exemplars, peer review, self-assessment, and mock events. Each of the four PCUs had a designated Clinical Nurse Specialist (CNS) who collaborated with their individual leadership team (manager, clinical leads, and advanced clinicians) to select the most applicable modality for evaluating competency, taking unit culture and patient population into consideration.

Outcome

This new innovative process for ongoing verification of competence produced a 600-hour reduction in non-productive time usage from 2011 to 2012 (1148 hours vs. 548 hours). See **Figure B.8** on the following page.

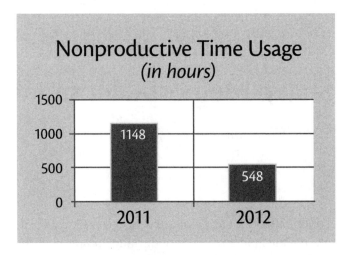

Figure B.8: Non-productive Time Usage

While the impetus for changing the competency assessment model was a desire to make the process more relevant and applicable to everyone involved, both cost-savings and educational benefits were realized. The new program allowed nursing staff to demonstrate their competence at the bedside via the modalities they felt best exemplified their knowledge and skill. Unit leadership was gratified by the new program which reduced employee non–productive time and therefore saved significant health care dollars. The cost savings of this innovative program was estimated at $25,320, based on a calculation of registered nurse average rate of pay and number of employee hours accumulated during the previous annual skills day.

Another positive outcome of using the Wright Competency Assessment Model was an increase in staff empowerment. Typically, nurse engagement improves when staff members are given the freedom to decide how best to demonstrate their knowledge and skill. Each PCU leadership team identified unit-specific competencies based on their culture and patient population which were relevant, meaningful, and educational, to further staff development. This commitment to the new competency validation process was recognized for its innovation and cost-saving benefits.

> *Both cost-savings and educational benefits came from changing our competency assessment model.*

RESULTS AND OUTCOMES

Summary

Donna Wright is known for using the terms "ownership, empowerment, and accountability" when incorporating her competency assessment model. If the staff are **empowered** to design their own work, their sense of **ownership** increases, and they become a group that exercises high **accountability**, not just at the task at hand, but elsewhere in their work as well.

Laurie Ecoff, PhD, RN, NEA-BC
Director Research, Education, Professional Practice

Janet Donnelly, MSN, RN-BC, ACNS-BC, PCCN
Clinical Nurse Specialist, Progressive Care Units

Lynn Marder, MS, RN, CCNS, PCCN
Clinical Nurse Specialist, Progressive Care Units

Sandy Nasshan, MSN, RN, PCCN
Clinical Nurse Specialist, Progressive Care Units

Belinda Toole, PhD(c), RN, CCNS, CCRN
Clinical Nurse Specialist, Progressive Care Units
Sharp Memorial Hospital

SECTION C

Tips for Implementing the Wright Competency Assessment Model

Where to Start

Our goals in transitioning to any new way of doing something are to make things better and to make the changes sustainable. Most of us have experienced "flavor of the month" changes in which we attempt to make a change, but it never really happens. Something inevitably gets us off track, and then we go on to the next shiny thing, and none of our efforts ever really takes hold. After working with lots and lots of organizations and helping them through transitions, here are some of my suggestions around implementing the Wright Competency Assessment Model.

Determining Where to Start

As you contemplate improving your competency assessment efforts, it is natural to start at what many of us think of, quite logically, as "the beginning." You may think it makes the most sense to start with the orientation competency process, getting that all cleaned up, and then move on to the ongoing competency process. Actually, I recommend the exact opposite. I recommend that you start with ongoing competencies first.

There are three main times when we do competency assessment: on hire, with initial orientation, and periodically/ongoing. See **Figure C.1** below.

Three categories of competency assessment:

Figure C.1: The Competency Continuum (Wright, 2005, pp. 17-19)

On-Hire Assessment

- Check licensure, registration, and certification

- Interview the potential candidate
- Check previous employment

Initial Competency (Orientation and Beyond)

The initial competency period will always include the following three components, whether it is formalized or not:

- Centralized orientation: Learning organizational aspects of the job
- Decentralized orientation: Time with a preceptor, mentor, or buddy learning department-specific aspects of the job
- Working independently while being closely supervised: Work assignments are given to the new employee who is periodically checked on and/or closely supervised

Ongoing/Periodic Competency

This includes assessing the ever-changing aspects of the job, specifically anything that is new, changing, high-risk, and/or problematic.

Why Start With the Ongoing Competency Process First?

One reality of orientation is this: no matter what you include in orientation, the final aspect that will make or break orientation is what the existing team members do to reinforce (or sabotage) what the new person was taught in orientation. All too often, on the person's first few days in the department, a new employee will hear something like, "I don't know what they told you in orientation, but we really don't do it like that here." As you have no doubt experienced, the existing team culture has a huge influence on the outcomes of any change we may try to incorporate. This is why I recommend that you start with the ongoing competency process. It's the attitudes and behaviors of your

> *It's the attitudes and behaviors of your existing team that have the biggest effect on culture, so they are the group you want to influence first with competency changes.*

TIPS FOR IMPLEMENTING THE WRIGHT COMPETENCY ASSESSMENT MODEL

existing team that have the biggest effect on culture, so they are the group you want to influence first.

My model emphasizes three elements: ownership, empowerment, and accountability. This model not only supports ways to identify and verify competencies more effectively; it sets in motion an infrastructure and culture that lift up ownership, empowerment, and accountability. I recommend that in the first year of implementation you focus on the ongoing competency process only. This way you can raise up those actions that create a culture that will align strongly with your organizational values and vision. I also highly recommend that you do not try to implement changes in both ongoing and initial competency at the same time.

Time and time again I see organizations try this, and it becomes very confusing for everyone involved in the process. I suggest starting with ongoing competency implementation in the first year. Then, after that gains a foothold, you can focus on the initial competency process. The only time I would suggest making changes to initial competencies while you are implementing the ongoing competency changes is when you are hiring a large number of people in one job class. Then you can revise the competency in that area. Just really try to focus the first year of implementation on the ongoing competency process only.

Ongoing Competency Assessment: Planning the Competency Cycle

When you're implementing this competency assessment process, it's important that for the first year you have a steering committee to guide the process. The competency steering committee has to address several basic things:

- The definition of competency

- Clarifying the competency cycle (particularly when it will begin and end)

- The roles that each person will play in the competency assessment process (the steering committee, the manager, the employee, the educator, HR, and other support staff)

There are several parts to the cycle:

Parts of the cycle:	Key person or group responsible:
1) Identify the competencies for each area.	Manager and some employees (educator and others can participate, but cannot do it for the manager and team). The team begins to "own" the competency assessment process by taking the lead in this step.
2) Select verification methods appropriate for the identified competencies.	Educator collaborates with team. Educator needs to be the in-house expert. Educator leads this action.
3) Allow staff sufficient time to bring the evidence forward to verify their competencies.	Employees are accountable to bring evidence forward (not the educator, not the manager—the employee!)
4) Aggregate the data regarding competency assessment for this time period.	Educator or manager or other designated person or group.

Figure C.2: Parts of the Competency Cycle

COMPETENCY ASSESSMENT FIELD GUIDE

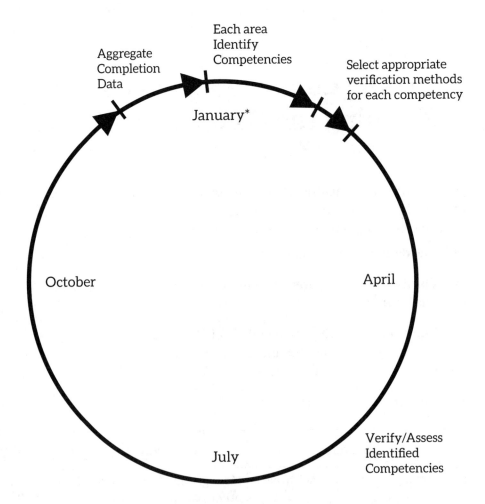

*In this diagram, January has been selected as a start date, just as an example. Your cycle can start and end at any point on the calendar.

Figure C.3: Example of a Typical Competency Cycle

Transition Planning: Implementing a Smooth Transition to Get Everyone on Board with the New Competency Model

Most transitions in implementing the Wright Model take one to two years. As you implement, keep in mind that this is more than "a way to do competency assessment." It is actually a shift and alignment of culture so that the daily culture moves in the same direction as your organizational values and vision. Take the time to make it right and sustainable. Take the time to implement with purpose.

Creating a Transition Plan

When you go from the old way of doing competency assessment to a new way of doing it, you need to have a transition plan. Here are some strategies to help you transition over a period of about two years. Keep in mind that this transition is not just about competency assessment and tracking; it is often a cultural shift in our thinking and doing. We are creating cultures that have a stronger focus on ownership, empowerment, and accountability.

Take some time to create a plan of action for the next two years. This transition plan should be created in the first 3-4 months of implementation. I suggest that you make this one of the first assignments given to a central competency steering committee or educator group: Clarify the organizational plan related to competency assessment.

COMPETENCY ASSESSMENT FIELD GUIDE

Assignment:

1. Map out your collective vision of the "dream" cycle for where you want to be two years from now.

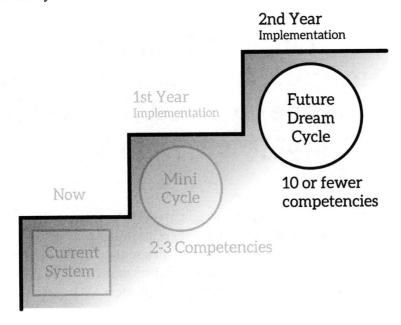

Figure C.4: Map out Dream Cycle

2. Reflect on your current organizational cycle or system for competency assessment.

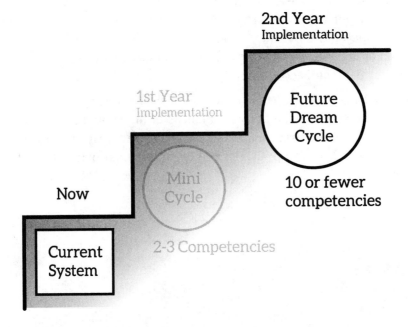

Figure C.5: Reflect on Current Cycle

TIPS FOR IMPLEMENTING THE WRIGHT COMPETENCY ASSESSMENT MODEL

3. Map out the bridge cycle for the new year that will help transition to this dream cycle.

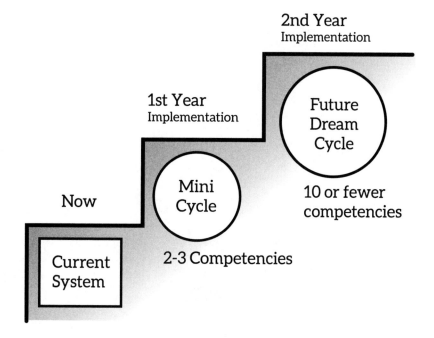

Figure C.6: Map out Bridge Cycle

4. When the cycles are identified, communicate the plan to all managers and educators multiple times, in multiple ways.

5. Create a plan to market this to all the employees. And again communicate it multiple times.

NOTE: When starting the first cycle, managers and educators should create competencies for themselves, along with staff competencies. These manager/educator competencies should focus on follow-up, consequences, not spoon-feeding, etc. We need to model the change we want to see in others.

Leadership Buy-in

How do you get leadership to buy in to the process?

This is a question I hear in almost every implementation of the Wright Competency Assessment Model. Most often this quest for leadership buy-in is focused on the executive level or other influential areas of the organization.

Here are several things to emphasize when you're trying to get buy-in from your leadership team.

Cost Savings

Cost savings is your number one leverage point. I have several organizations reporting significant cost savings with my competency model. This is mostly due to the use of evidence-based verification methods or in-practice outcomes, rather than the "line people up and check them off" approach, which can be very costly. One organization in San Diego reported saving over $25,000 in one department with their competency effort in just their first year of implementation. (See page 167.)

Improvement in Quality Outcomes

This competency model helps align all of your actions with the organization's strategic goals for the year. Because my model has such a strong tie to Quality Improvement (QI) measurement, and QI is almost always aligned with the organization's strategic goals, competency is a great way to get every employee moving in that same direction and achieve your outcomes. Because the Wright Model of Competency Assessment results in greater employee ownership, empowerment, and accountability, outcome data such as ventilator-associated pneumonia, falls, nosocomial infections, etc., should improve. You will find a wonderful case study that illustrates this kind of outcome improvement related to fall rates from an organization in Billings, Montana, on page 131. This model purposefully aligns your competency process with your strategic goals and objectives as well as your balanced scorecard data.

Identification of Low Performers and Recognition of High Performers

The Wright Model of Competency Assessment can identify and address the low performers, while also recognizing the high performers. Almost all employees like this competency model better than the previous approach. They have more control in the selection and measurement of competencies, which leads to a greater sense of ownership and increased staff satisfaction. The only groups that do not like this model are employees who are low performers trying to fly below the radar and/or those who have chronic excuses for their lower-than-desired performance. They do not like this competency model, because it invariably exposes their lack of skill and/or commitment.

> *The only groups that do not like this model are employees who are low performers trying to fly below the radar and/or those who have chronic excuses for their lower-than-desired performance.*

On the other hand, those employees who are doing a great job often say that this method of competency assessment makes them feel more recognized for their work. The exemplars and evidence-based measurements make them feel proud to work at their organization, and they feel more "seen" in their routine outcomes. This is no small thing. Databases such as the US Bureau of Labor and Statistics have shown time and time again that recognition is one of the leading indicators for retention. This competency model brings greater illumination to recognition of high performers, which will lead to retaining these great professionals who contribute to positive outcomes and overall organizational culture.

The Wright Competency Model: What it Takes to Bring it to Life

Here are some basic aspects of successful operationalization of the Wright Competency Assessment Model. These are key actions that will help achieve your goals and create sustainable results. This is kind of a "to-do" list to help you plan what you'll do.

Understand the Model and Introduce it to Others

Introduce the concept of the model to your team. Most groups start with their educators or other current competency champions. Some have formed book clubs and reviewed the model together as a group.

Then expose the manager group to the model. I recommend a workshop for managers and educators to give them an overview of the model. Actually this competency model is far more than just a competency strategy; it is a great leadership strategy for managers as well. It is not just about assessing and tracking competency; this model helps you to lead your team, manage low performers, recognize high performers, and align your efforts more directly with your organization's values and strategic goals. Introducing managers to this competency model will give them leadership skills they can use right away. This is a good investment, especially for middle manager groups.

1. **Form a steering committee.**

    A steering committee is necessary for the first year or so of your transition to the Wright Model of Competency Assessment. The steering committee can be an existing group that takes on the responsibility, or it can be a new group that will map out the rollout plan. This group should immediately take on the tasks of defining competency assessment for the organization (regulatory groups ask you to do this) and creating a cycle that will guide your competency assessment activities. (See "Ongoing Competency Assessment: Planning the Competency Cycle" on page 177 for cycle suggestions.)

2. **Start with ongoing competencies first.**

   Start with the ongoing competency cycle first, rather than with the initial and orientation competency strategies. Ongoing competencies have a bigger impact on the team and, therefore, the success of the overall competency model transformation. If you start with initial competencies, you can do a great deal of work for very little return, and the existing team members can easily kill the outcomes by saying, "I don't know what they told you in orientation, but we don't really do it like that here." (See "Where to Start" on page 173 for further information.)

   > *If you start with initial competencies, you can do a great deal of work for very little return, and the existing team members can easily kill the outcomes by saying, "I don't know what they told you in orientation, but we don't really do it like that here."*

3. **Make time for evaluation, reflection, and ongoing staff input.**

   Implementation of this competency model generally takes one to two years. It is important to include evaluation and reflection in this process at the end of year one, but also throughout subsequent years. Make sure leaders and employees know who they can give input to; include contact information for relevant people and groups so that feedback can flow easily as the transition unfolds. This will make your implementation process fit your organization and its personality. Every group I have worked with implements this model slightly differently. Make it your own, and customize the process for success.

Competently Go . . .

Competency assessment is far more than just checking someone off for a skill!

Competency assessment is . . .

- A way to articulate the ever-changing expectations of the job and the organizational vision
- A way to create ownership of practice and service
- A method to focus action and response to achieve quality outcomes
- A strategy to recognize high performers as well as to assess and direct low performers
- A strategy to measure engagement and commitment
- A vehicle to create empowerment

This competency model can help you create ownership, empowerment, and accountability, which in turn facilitate alignment with your organization's goals. In the end, you are not just assessing competency; you are aligning your thoughts and actions for better patient outcomes and a healthy environment based on critical thinking, reflection, and accountability. Most organizations have said that this model did much more than just shape competencies; it helped increase employee engagement and shared governance and decrease overall costs. This model takes some investment of thought and time, but the return on investment is well worth it.

Personally, what I love in this competency assessment work is helping people create something that gives them more than they ever dreamt of before. Most people tell me they are drowning in their competency assessment process. They have created a monster they can't live with anymore. They have lists and lists of competencies that have accumulated over the years. I get so excited when I can help people create a process that helps them to clarify their future and to shape competencies and assessment processes to realize that future. With a world that is changing all the time, a dynamic competency process is a gift we give ourselves. And on top of all this, we help increase ownership, empowerment, and accountability along the way. It doesn't get better than that!

Competently go . . . where no one has gone before!

Special Thanks
to those Who Chose to Boldly Go into a New World of Competency Assessment

Julie Bane, MS, RN-BC
  Clinical Education Specialist
  Arkansas Children's Hospital, Little Rock, Arkansas. 145

Carla Borchardt, MS, RN, NE-BC
  Director of Professional Practice and Magnet® Program Director
  Avera McKennan Hospital & University Health Center, Sioux Falls,
  South Dakota 121

Deborah A. Combs, BSN, RN
  Specialty Educator
  Morton Plant Hospital, Clearwater, Florida. 115

Sharon Conway, MSN, RN, NE-BC
  Director, Patient Care Operations
  Norton Healthcare, Louisville, Kentucky 81

Annette Dailey, MSN, RN
  KHN Learning System Manager
  Kettering Behavioral Health Center, Kettering, Ohio 73

Ellen Derry, MA, BSN, RN-BC, CPN
  Director, Education and Professional Development
  Virginia Commonwealth University Health System, Richmond, Virginia . . 101

Carol Dimura, MSN, RNC
  Clinical Education Coordinator for Staff Development
  Morton Plant Mease HealthCare (part of BayCare Health System),
  Clearwater, Florida 105

Janet Donnelly, MSN, RN-BC, ACNS-BC, PCCN
  Clinical Nurse Specialist, Progressive Care Units
  Sharp Memorial Hospital, San Diego, California 167

Laurie Ecoff, PhD, RN, NEA-BC
Director Research, Education, Professional Practice
Sharp Memorial Hospital, San Diego, California 167

Solimar Figueroa, MSN, MHA, BSN, RN
Clinical Educator-Clinical Learning
Baptist Health South Florida, Miami, Florida 161

Michele Fix, MSN, RN, NE-BC
Manager of Clinical Informatics & Practice
Children's Mercy Hospital, Kansas City, Missouri 95

Kitty Hancock, MSN, RN
Nurse Educator
Charles George Veterans Affairs Medical Center,
Asheville, North Carolina 153

Barbara Johns, MHA, BSN, RN
Clinical Education Specialist
Arkansas Children's Hospital, Little Rock, Arkansas..................... 145

Michele Kelly, RN, MSN,
Executive Director of Quality
Buena Vista Regional Medical Center, Storm Lake, Iowa 69

Ellen Kisling, MSN, RN
Director of Education
Children's Mercy Hospital, Kansas City, Missouri 95

Michele Kolp, MSN, RN
Nursing Professional Development Specialist
Kettering Behavioral Health Center, Kettering, Ohio 73

Michelle Lane, MSN, RN, CMSRN, NE-BC
Nursing Education Manager
North Kansas City Hospital, North Kansas City, Missouri.................. 85

Walter Lewanowicz, MN, BSc, RN-BC
Nurse Educator, Department of Education & Professional Development
Virginia Commonwealth University Health System, Richmond, Virginia .. 101

Paula Lewis, RN-C, BSN, MBA
Program Manager, Clinical Learning
St. Luke's Health System, Boise, Idaho.................................... 89

SPECIAL THANKS

Lynn Marder, MS, RN, CCNS, PCCN
    Clinical Nurse Specialists, Progressive Care Units
    Sharp Memorial Hospital, San Diego, California 167

Felisha Mason, MSN, RN, CPN
    Clinical Education Specialist
    Arkansas Children's Hospital, Little Rock, Arkansas..................... 145

Sandy Nasshan, MSN, RN, PCCN
    Clinical Nurse Specialist, Progressive Care Units
    Sharp Memorial Hospital, San Diego, California 167

Susan Regan O'Brien, MS, BS
    Education Consultant, Education Department
    Waterbury Hospital, Waterbury, Connecticut 61

Mary Rogers, MSN, RN, CNOR
    Clinical Education Coordinator
    Fairfield Medical Center, Lancaster, Ohio................................. 137

Rose Schaffer, MS, RN
    Staff Development Specialist
    Lawrence Memorial Hospital, Lawrence, Kansas 65

Michele Schwister, PICU RN, BSN, CCRN
    Bedside Nurse, Relief Charge, Chair of the Education Committee
    St. Luke's Children's Center, Boise, Idaho 93

Cherry R Shogren, MSN, RN, NE-BC
    Director, Clinical Professional Development
    UnityPoint Health Des Moines, Des Moines, Iowa.........................77

Christine Sites, MSN, RN
    Nursing Professional Development Specialist
    University of Pennsylvania Hospital, Philadelphia, Pennsylvania 125

Laurie Smith, MSN, RN, CEN, CNML
    Manager ATU
    Billings Clinic, Billings, Montana 131

Donna Steigleder, BSN, RN
    Director of Employee Relations
    Virginia Commonwealth University Health System,
    Richmond, Virginia 101

Jennifer Tafelmeyer, BSN, RN, PCCN
    Clinical Coordinator ATU
    Billings Clinic, Billings, Montana 131

Belinda Toole, PhD(c), RN, CCNS, CCRN
    Clinical Nurse Specialist, Progressive Care Units
    Sharp Memorial Hospital, San Diego, California 167

Doris Van Dyke, BSN, RN-BC
    Nursing Education Specialist
    Robert Wood Johnson University Hospital at Somerset,
    Somerville, New Jersey 117

Lametria Wafford, MNSc, RN-BC
    Clinical Education Specialist
    Arkansas Children's Hospital, Little Rock, Arkansas..................... 145

Tammy Webb, MS, RN, NE-BC
    Vice President Acute Care
    Arkansas Children's Hospital, Little Rock, Arkansas..................... 145

Robin Wicks, MSN, RN, PCCN
    ATU Clinician
    Billings Clinic, Billings, Montana 131

References

Benner, P. (2001). *From novice to expert: Excellence and power in clinical nursing practice.* New York: Prentice Hall.

Drenkard, K. (2010, June). The business case for Magnet®. *Journal of Nursing Administration, 40*(6), pp. 263-271.

Eckerd College. (2014). CDP-Individual Leadership Development Institute. Retrieved from www.conflictdynamics.org

Gawande, A. (2010). *The checklist manifesto.* New York: Picador.

Hines P. A. & Yu K.M. (2009, January-February). The changing reimbursement landscape: Nurses' role in quality and operational excellence. *Nursing Economics, 27*(1), pp. 1-7.

Swanson, K. (1991). Empirical development of a middle range theory of caring. *Nursing Research, 40*(3), 161.166.

Vernon, R., Chiarella, M., & Papps, E. (2013). Assessing the continuing competence of nurses in New Zealand. *Journal of Nursing Regulation, 3*(4).

Webb, T, & Walker, W. (2012). Arkansas Children's Hospital: A framework for education and professional development. In D. Bradley, (Ed.), Scope and Standards [column]. *Journal for Nurses in Staff Development,* 297-299.

Wright, D. (2013). Competency programs. In S. Bruce (Ed.), Core *Curriculum for Nursing Professional Development* (4th Ed.). (pp. 499-513). Chicago, IL: Association for Nursing Professional Development.

Wright, D. (2004, January/February). Is education the answer? *Trendlines.* Pensacola, FL: National Nursing Staff Development Organization.

Wright, D. (2004, June/July). Is education the answer? - Part 2 *Trendlines.* Pensacola, FL: National Nursing Staff Development Organization.

Wright, D. (2005). *The ultimate guide to competency assessment in health care.* Minneapolis, MN: Creative Health Care Management.

Wright, D. (2014). *The Wright model of competency assessment.* DVD. Minneapolis, MN: Creative Health Care Management.

Index

Abbreviation "WCAM" stands for Wright Competency Assessment Model.

accountability
    about the principle of, 5–6, 175, 187–88
    changing the culture, 101–04, 123–24
    competency assessment and, 49–53, 161–66
    competency validation, 105–13
    defined/described, 8–9
    focus on work and outcomes, 47, 61–62, 121–24, 131–35
    implementing a new model, 77–79, 81–84
    misconceptions vs. reality, 2–3
    regulatory standards, 13
    role of validators, 35–37
    shifting the paradigm, 95–99
    skill fairs and, 106, 115–16
    staff participation and empowerment, 73–75, 85–88, 125–28, 183–84
    See also Wright Competency Assessment Model
Arkansas Children's Hospital (Little Rock, AR), 145–51
automated data collection. *See* documentation/data collection
automatic skills/behaviors. *See* high-risk skills
Avera McKennan Hospital & University Health Center (Sioux Falls, SD), 121–24

Baptist Health South Florida (Miami, FL), 161–66
BayCare Health System (Clearwater, FL), 105–13
Benner, Patricia, 82, 139, 162
Billings Clinic (Billings, MT), 131–35
Buena Vista Regional Medical Center (Storm Lake, IA), 69–71

cardiopulmonary resuscitation (CPR), 13, 26, 107–08
case studies, stories from the field incorporating WCAM principles
    Avera McKennan Hospital & University Health Center (Sioux Falls, SD), 121–24
    Buena Vista Regional Medical Center (Storm Lake, IA), 69–71
    Children's Mercy Hospital (Kansas City, MO), 95–99
    Kettering Behavioral Medical Center (Kettering, OH), 73–75
    Lawrence Memorial Hospital (Lawrence, KS), 65–67
    Morton Plant Hospital (Clearwater, FL), 115–16
    Morton Plant Mease Health Care (Clearwater, FL), 105–13
    North Kansas City Hospital (North Kansas City, MO), 85–88
    Norton Healthcare (Louisville, KY), 81–84
    Robert Wood Johnson University Hospital (Somerville, NJ), 117–20
    St. Luke's Children's Hospital (Boise, ID), 93–94
    St. Luke's Health System (Boise, ID), 89–92
    UnityPoint Health Des Moines (Des Moines, IA), 77–79
    University of Pennsylvania Health System (Philadelphia, PA), 125–28
    Virginia Commonwealth University Health System (Richmond, VA), 101–04
    Waterbury Hospital (Waterbury, CT), 61–64
    See also Wright Competency Assessment Model
case studies, results and outcomes
    Arkansas Children's Hospital (Little Rock, AR), 145–51

Baptist Health South Florida (Miami, FL), 161–66
Billings Clinic (Billings, MT), 131–35
Charles George Veterans Affairs Medical Center (Asheville, NC), 153–59
Fairfield Medical Center (Lancaster, OH), 137–44
Sharp Memorial Hospital (San Diego, CA), 167–69
Centers for Medicare and Medicaid Services (CMS), 13
Charles George Veterans Affairs Medical Center (Asheville, NC), 153–59
The Checklist Manifesto (Gwande), 23–24
checklists
    competency assessment using, 23–24
    high-risk/low volume skills, 26–27
    misconceptions vs. reality, 2, 153
    replaced by WCAM, 63, 69–71, 101–02, 140
    technical skills, 137
"checky, checky, checky," 82
Children's Mercy Hospital (Kansas City, MO), 95–99
"code violet." *See* restraint competencies
commitment. *See* engagement and commitment
Competency Assessment Model. *See* Wright Competency Assessment Model
Competency Assessment Roadtrip (CAR), 95–99
Competency Continuum, 173
Competency Cycle, 177–78
competency validation
    accountability, 95–98, 158
    adapting to new technology, 70
    creating a WCAM model, 107–13, 121–24, 133–35
    documentation, 82
    implementing a new model, 137–44, 164–66
    overcoming inconsistency, 81
    overcoming inefficiency, 77–78
    overcoming stagnation, 85, 101–04
    staff empowerment and participation, 73–74, 91–92, 125–28, 168
    standardization, 71
    unit-based vs. central skills lab, 117–20
    See also validators
computers. *See* electronic record keeping; web-based application
consensus decision-making, 158
costs/cost-savings
    achieving with WCAM, 57, 93–94, 168, 187–88
    competency validation, 119
    high-risk/low volume skills, 26
    hospitalization, 134–35
    leveraging leadership buy-in, 183–84
    skill fairs, 85
    use of validators, 35
crisis management, 20–21
critical thinking skill. *See* skills, mastery/maintenance
cyclical assessment, 41–42

del Bueno, Dorothy, 139, 162
documentation/data collection
    checklists, 23–24
    competency assessment, 95–98, 153–55
    competency validation, 36–37, 69–71, 82–84, 101–03
    developing templates, 163–66
    electronic vs. paper, 45–47, 125
    identifying requirements, 127–28
    job descriptions, 39–40
    overcoming challenges, 127–28
    overcoming resistance, 116
    performance review/appraisal, 41–42
    regulatory compliance, 13–15
    See also electronic record keeping; tracking

education
    avoiding "spray and pray" approach, 29–31
    determining desired outcomes, 33–34
    nursing core competencies, 81–84
    professional development initiatives, 145–51
    resistance to change, 119
    response to performance issues, 30, 52, 132
    shifting the paradigm, 85–88

INDEX

electronic record keeping, 45–46, 64, 82
    See also documentation/data collection
employee evaluation. *See* performance management
employee retention, 184
empowerment
    about the principle of, 5–6, 175, 187–88
    competency assessment and, 49–53
    creating a new model, 179–81
    defined/described, 8–9
    developing validation methodology, 73–75
    See also Wright Competency Assessment Model
engagement and commitment
    competency assessment and, 49–53, 187–88
    competency validation, 107–08
    competency verification, 5–8
    consensus decision-making, 158
    improvements in accountability, 95–99, 121–24, 128, 133–34
    improvements in education, 147–51
    outcomes assessment, 142–43
    overcoming challenges, 110–11
    recognizing cost savings, 93–94
    recognizing time savings, 119–20
    recognizing WCAM success, 62, 66, 73–74, 83–84, 91–94
Evaluating Training Programs (Kirkpatrick), 150
evaluation
    about WCAM and, 78, 89–91
    assessing competencies, 41–42, 101–03, 167–69
    education initiatives, 145–51
    implementing WCAM, 138–44, 185–86
    precepting and orientation, 35–36
    standardization, 43
    See also performance management
exemplar statements, 102, 154, 156–59
external regulatory standards, 14

facility-specific competencies, 81–84
Fairfield Medical Center (Lancaster, OH), 137–44

float pool
    about the relevant competencies, 17–18
    crisis management options, 20–21
    learning on the fly, 18–19
    positive vs. negative marketing, 19–20

Gwande, Atul, 23–24

high-risk skills
    checklist protocols, 24
    dynamics of change, 39–40, 147–48
    establishing organizational policy, 14–15
    insuring competent action, 25–27
    motivation for change, 62, 85–86, 101–02, 161–62, 173–74

initial competency assessment, 173–75
internal organizational policy, 14–16
Internet. *See* web-based applications
interpersonal skills. *See* skills, mastery/maintenance

job descriptions, 39–40, 61–63, 70, 125
The Joint Commission (TJC), 13, 63, 82, 101–03, 137

Kettering Behavioral Medical Center (Kettering, OH), 73–75
Kirkpatrick, Donald, 150

Lawrence Memorial Hospital (Lawrence, KS), 65–67
"learning on the fly" competency, 18–19

mandatory competencies
    about the WCAM and, 5
    evolution from policies to expectation, 14
    implementing change, 69–70, 89–92, 113, 126
    misconceptions vs. reality, 1–4
    resorting to "spray and pray" tactics, 29–31
    rethinking the education module, 131–34, 145–46, 161–64
marketing your competencies, 19–20

misconceptions vs. reality, competency assessment, 1–4
mistakes and errors, analyzing, 29–31
Morton Plant Hospital (Clearwater, FL), 115–16
Morton Plant Mease Health Care (Clearwater, FL), 105–08

National Database of Nursing Quality Indicators (NDNQI), 134
"No Spoon Feeding," 8–9, 86, 105, 112, 181
North Kansas City Hospital (North Kansas City, MO), 85–88
Norton Healthcare (Louisville, KY), 82–84
"Novice to Expert Theory" (Benner, 2005), 82, 139
nursing
    core competencies, 81–84
    practice model, 65–67, 125
    shift to unit-based validation, 117–20
    shifting the accountability paradigm, 121–24

ongoing competency assessment, 173–75
on-hire assessment, 173–74
on-line application. *See* web-based applications
outcomes. *See* Wright Competency Assessment Model, results and outcomes
outcomes tracking, 29, 43
ownership
    about the principle of, 5–6, 175, 187–88
    competency assessment and, 49–53
    creating a new model, 179–81
    defined/described, 6–8
    focus on work and outcomes, 47
    See also Wright Competency Assessment Model

partners-in-practice model, 20–21
patient safety, 37, 64, 86, 95–97, 105–08, 118, 146–51, 154–55
performance management
    articulating expectations, 9, 39–40, 42, 43, 51, 87
    identifying high/low performers, 184
    performance review, 41–42, 63, 69

    See also evaluation
periodic competency assessment, 173–75
position-specific competency, 154–55
positive vs. negative attitude, float pool, 19–20
preceptor/precepting and orientation, 35, 111–12, 153–54, 174. *See also* validators
prioritization
    adjusting to changing requirements, 101
    applying WCAM, 91
    creating staff unity, 125–28
    education initiatives, 146
    misconceptions vs. reality, 3
    resulting in decreased costs, 151

Quality Improvement (QI), 183
quality monitoring, 43

reality check, debunking misconceptions, 1–4
regulations and standards
    about the regulatory bodies, 13–14
    external standards, 14
    internal organizational policy, 14–16
Relationship-Based Care (RBC), 65–66
restraint competencies, 3–4, 14–16, 73–74, 121, 155
return demonstration, 23, 26, 36, 101–02, 118–19
Robert Wood Johnson University Hospital (Somerville, NJ), 117–20

Sharp Memorial Hospital (San Diego, CA), 167–69
Six Sigma, 113, 140
skills, mastery/maintenance
    applying WCAM to, 5–9
    checklists, 23–24
    developing consistency, 69–71
    education, as solution to performance, 85–88
    education, regulatory requirements, 81–84
    implementing a competency "makeover," 137–44
    implementing nursing practice model, 65–67

implementing WCAM, 90–91, 133, 161–62, 187–88
misconceptions vs. reality, 1–4
process/timing of assessment, 102–03
validators, 35–37
verification methods, 154–56
skills fair
    applying WCAM, 62
    creating a fair that works, 115–16
    drawbacks/problems, 105–06, 126–28
    education vs. validation, 122
    high-risk skills competency, 26–27
    maintaining regulatory standards, 14
    role of validators, 36
    unit-based competency vs., 117–20, 166
"Slaying the Competency Monster" conference (Wright), 95
specialty-specific competencies, 81–84
spoon-feeding, 8–9, 86, 105, 112, 181
"spray and pray" education, 29–31
St. Luke's Children's Hospital (Boise, ID), 93–94
St. Luke's Health System (Boise, ID), 89–92
standardization
    about the competency process, 43
    competency validation, 71, 105–08
    job descriptions, 63
    overcoming fragmentation and inconsistency, 69–71
    overcoming inefficiency, 77
Swanson's Theory of Caring, 82
Swihart, Diana, 162

talent management products. *See* tracking
technical skill. *See* skills, mastery/maintenance
time-sensitive competencies, 24–27, 117–20, 155, 161
Tobin, Mike, 140
total patient care, 20–21
tracking
    applying WCAM is more than, 185–86
    collecting and storing data, 45–47
    education and regulatory requirements, 117–20, 145–46
    employee evaluation, 41–42

    incorporating into transition planning, 179–80
    project tasks/progress, 64
    standardization, 43
    See also documentation/data collection
    transition planning, 179–81

The Ultimate Guide to Competency Assessment in Health Care (Wright), 30, 67, 122, 128, 138–40
UnityPoint Health Des Moines (Des Moines, IA), 77–79
University of Pennsylvania Health System (Philadelphia, PA), 125–28

validators, 24, 35–37, 118
    See also competency validation; preceptor/precepting and orientation
verification methods
    about WCAM and, 8–9
    checklists, 23–24
    choice of methods, 154–55
    creating accountability, 121–24
    creating consistency/standards, 77–79, 82–84, 96–98, 125–28
    employee responsibility, 52–53
    evaluating performance standards, 85–88
    time constraints, 110
    using validators, 35–37
Virginia Commonwealth University Health System (Richmond, VA), 101–04

Waterbury Hospital (Waterbury, CT), 61–64
web-based applications, 63–64, 70, 81, 86, 118–19, 125, 132
    See also electronic record keeping
webinars, 91, 122
Wright Competency Assessment Model (WCAM)
    about the principles, 5–9
    changing the meaning of competency, 89–92
    competency validation enhancement, 105–08
    cost-savings, 93–94, 134, 167–69
    creating a change in culture, 61–64

creating effective skills fairs, 115–16
developing a nursing practice model, 65–67, 125
education, shifting the paradigm, 85–88
nursing core competencies, 81–84
overcoming fragmentation and inconsistency, 69–71
staff participation and empowerment, 73–75, 125–28
standardization, 77–79
unit-based validation, 117–20
See also accountability; case studies; empowerment; ownership

Wright Competency Assessment Model, results and outcomes
creating a new assessment process, 137–44
developing consistency and complexity compression, 145–51
developing ongoing competencies, 153–59
education, costs and time-savings, 167–69
focus on competency vs. process, 161–66
strategies impacting, 131–35

Wright Competency Assessment Model, tips for implementing
assessment, where to begin, 173–75
planning the competency cycle, 177–78
planning the transition period, 179–81
securing leadership buy-in, 183–84
"to-do" list to start the process, 185–86

The Ultimate Guide to Competency Assessment in Health Care, 3rd Edition

Have you created a "monster" with your competency assessment process that you don't want to live with anymore? Are you ready to move your competency assessment process beyond just meeting regulatory standards to creating excellence? Donna Wright's creative approach to competency assessment creates ownership, empowerment, and accountability in your staff, and at the same time saves money, decreases assessment time, and has a noticeable positive impact on outcomes.

The Ultimate Guide to Competency Assessment in Health Care is packed with ready-to-use tools designed to help you and your staff develop, implement, and evaluate competencies. This book will offer you a new way of thinking about competency assessment—a way that is outcome-focused and accountability-based. With over 35,000 copies sold world-wide, it is the most trusted resource on competency assessment available.

Softcover, 232 pages. (2005) – B1051B, $34.95

The Wright Model of Competency Assessment DVD

Join Donna Wright as she delivers an informative overview of Donna Wright's Competency Assessment Model. In just 25 short minutes you will gain the basics of this process. Executives love this quick overview.

This model is being used all over the world. And this video will give you the basic concepts to get your thinking wheels moving in better, more creative ways with your competency assessment process.

Objectives:
- Learn the goal of competency assessment and the driving forces behind the process
- Discover how to promote accountability through competency assessment
- Learn the factors that help make competency assessment truly successful

DVD, 25 minutes. (2014) – V315-DVD, $24.95

Competency Assessment Services

Organizations are required by regulatory bodies to implement a system for ongoing assessment of competencies related to staff job functions. Many organizations have made this process far more cumbersome and time consuming than it needs to be, and in the process, they've missed an opportunity for competency assessment to be highly developmental and truly inspiring.

CHCM consultant Donna Wright is the country's foremost authority on competency assessment. Maybe it's time to learn a better approach to competency assessment that will not only meet the regulatory standards while promoting accountability, but will teach, inspire, and deliver results.

Professional Development Services

Our team of highly skilled and sought after experts can help deepen individual and organizational knowledge and abilities to meet the ever-changing health care environment. We offer services that help you create the structures and processes that will deliver the outcomes your organization is looking for.

The experience and talent of our professional development consultants are unmatched in the industry. Our experts partner with you to develop customized consultation support. We provide professional development in mission, vision, and values; strategic planning; structure and restructuring, resource assessment and evaluation, and precepting and mentoring programs.

Visit: chcm.com or call 800.728.7766 for more information about how Creative Health Care Management can help with your competency assessment and professional development needs.

When Creative Health Care Management spends time consulting in your organization, we lay the foundation for ongoing success.

CHCM's well-rounded, solution-minded professional development team helps maximize your team's capacity, satisfaction, and performance. We have our finger on the pulse of national best practices and a long track record of knowing what works.

The experience and talent of our professional development consultants are unmatched in the industry. Our experts partner with you to develop customized consultation support. We provide professional development in mission, vision, and values; strategic planning; structure and restructuring; resource assessment and evaluation, and precepting and mentoring programs. We offer services that help you create the structures and processes that will deliver the outcomes your organization is looking for.

CHCM's Competency & Professional Development team members are known for their ability to captivate and motivate audiences in a variety of venues from one-hour to week-long educational activities.

ORDER FORM

1. Order Online at: shop.chcm.com.
2. Call toll-free 800.728.7766 x4 and use your Visa, Mastercard, American Express, Discover, or a company purchase order.
3. Fax your order to: 952.854.1866.
4. Mail your order with pre-payment or company purchase order to:

   Creative Health Care Management
   6200 Baker Road, Suite 200
   Minneapolis, MN 55346
   Attn: Resources Department

Product	Price	Quantity	Subtotal	TOTAL
B655—*Competency Assessment Field Guide*	$34.95			
B1051B—*The Ultimate Guide to Competency Assessment in Health Care*	$34.95			
V315—*DVD: The Wright Model of Competency Assessment*	$24.95			
V310—*The Ultimate Guide to Preceptoring Video Series*	$199.00			
V305PS—*The Moments of Excellence Video Series*	$199.00			
B510—*Relationship-Based Care: A Model for Transforming Practice*	$34.95			
Shipping Costs: Please call 800.728.7766 x4 for a shipping estimate.				
Order TOTAL				

Need more than one copy? We have quantity discounts available.

Quantity Discounts		
10–49 = 10% off	50–99 = 20% off	100 or more = 30% off

Payment Methods: ☐ Credit Card ☐ Check ☐ Purchase Order PO# _____

Credit Card	Number	Expiration	AVS (3 digits)
Visa / Mastercard / AMEX / Discover	– – –	/	

Cardholder address (if different from below):   Signature:

Customer Information	
Name:	
Title:	
Company:	
Address:	
City, State, Zip:	
Daytime Phone:	
Email:	

Satisfaction guarantee: If you are not satisfied with your purchase, simply return the products within 30 days for a full refund.
For a free catalog of all our products, visit www.chcm.com or call 800.728.7766 x4.